DIETRICH BONHOEFFER

Makers of the Modern Theological Mind
Bob E. Patterson, Editor

KARL BARTH by *David L. Mueller*
DIETRICH BONHOEFFER by *Dallas M. Roark*
RUDOLF BULTMANN by *Morris Ashcraft*
CHARLES HARTSHORNE by *Alan Gragg*
WOLFHART PANNENBERG by *Don Olive*

Makers of the Modern Theological Mind
Bob E. Patterson, Editor

DIETRICH BONHOEFFER

by Dallas M. Roark

Word Books, Publisher, Waco, Texas

First Printing—July 1972
Second Printing—January 1975
Third Printing—April 1975
Fourth Printing—December 1975

DIETRICH BONHOEFFER

Library of Congress catalog card number: 72-76439

Printed in the United States of America

To
Elaine
and
Lyman and Dalaine

Contents

EDITOR'S PREFACE 9

PREFACE 11

I. DIETRICH BONHOEFFER: THE MAN AND HIS INTERPRETERS 13

Bonhoeffer the Man • 13
The Interpreters of Bonhoeffer • 25

II. THE SHAPE OF THE CHURCH 30

Defining Sociology and the Church • 30
What the Church Is • 33

III. THE CHURCH: OBJECTIVE SOURCE OF REVELATION 38

The Alternatives of Philosophy • 38
The Problem Stated for Theology • 41
Bonhoeffer's Solution • 42

IV. THE CHURCH SEEKING TO KNOW ITSELF 45

Questions about Christ • 45
Wrong Answers about Christ • 48
Lectures on Genesis • 50
Practical Advice on Temptation • 57

V. THE CHURCH'S LIFE IN CHRIST 62

The Christian Community • 62
The Community at Worship • 64
Personal Worship • 67
Types of Ministries • 68
A Proposal for a Protestant Confessional • 71

VI. THE CHURCH'S BRAND OF
DISCIPLESHIP 75

What Is Discipleship? • 75
The Sermon on the Mount • 80
Discipleship Today • 86

VII. THE CHURCH CONFRONTING THE
WORLD 93

The Uniqueness of Christian Ethics • 93
Ethical Issues • 100
What It Means to Be Real • 101
The Mandates • 105
A Miscellany of Essays • 107

VIII. THE CHURCH AGAINST RELIGION 114

IX. THE SIGNIFICANCE OF BONHOEFFER .. 123

The Man • 123
The Theological Revolution • 125
Areas of Significance • 126

FOOTNOTES 131

SELECTED BIBLIOGRAPHY 140

Editor's Preface

Who are the thinkers that have shaped Christian theology in our time? This series tries to answer that question by providing a reliable guide to the ideas of the men who have significantly charted the theological seas of our century. In the current revival of theology, these books will give a new generation the opportunity to be exposed to significant minds. They are not meant, however, to be a substitute for a careful study of the original works of these makers of the modern theological mind.

This series is not for the lazy. Each major theologian is examined carefully and critically—his life, his theological method, his most germinal ideas, his weaknesses as a thinker, his place in the theological spectrum, and his chief contribution to the climate of theology today. The books are written with the assumption that laymen will read them and enter into the theological dialogue that is so necessary to the church as a whole. At the same time they are carefully enough designed to give assurance to a Ph.D. student in theology preparing for his preliminary exams.

Each author in the series is a professional scholar and theologian in his own right. All are specialists on, and in some cases have studied with, the theologians about whom they write. Welcome to the series.

BOB E. PATTERSON, Editor
Baylor University

Preface

An invitation to do a short work on Bonhoeffer was an opportunity for me to dig deeper into this brilliant theologian. This work will not command the attention of the devotee of Bonhoeffer. It is designed to give the reader a quick snapshot view of the man, his life and thought. If I have succeeded in doing this, I will have more than passed my hopeful expectations.

There are always numerous people that help in making a book possible. First on the list is Dr. Bob Patterson of Baylor University, who serves as the General Editor of this series. His kindness in asking me places me in debt to him. A special word of gratitude goes to various library resources: The library of the College of Emporia, the library of the United Christian Fellowship, and the William Allen White Library. These libraries have been patient with me although I had several of their books over a period of some months.

As usual, an author owes gratitude to his wife and children while he removes his presence from their activities, and this one is no exception. Thus I must dedicate this work to my wife, Elaine, and my two loving children, Lyman and Dalaine.

—DALLAS M. ROARK

I. Dietrich Bonhoeffer:
The Man and His Interpreters

BONHOEFFER THE MAN

Dietrich Bonhoeffer has become a man with mystique. His life commands intense interest because of his opposition to the Nazi state and its infiltration of the German church. His theological works remain a source of inspiration not only for his vivid exposition of profound issues, but also for the well-turned phrases such as "cheap grace" or "world come of age." His involvement in the ecumenical movement as a young theologian brought immense respect from older and better known men. Whether Bonhoeffer has been interpreted rightly is still debated, but no one doubts that he has had a remarkable influence in contemporary Protestant theology.

Dietrich and his twin sister Sabine were born on February 4, 1906, in Breslau, Germany (which is now part of Poland). His mother was descended from the famous nineteenth-century church historian, Karl von Hase, and his father, Karl Ludwig Bonhoeffer, was a noted physician and soon to be professor of psychiatry at the University of Berlin. The fact that his father distrusted Freudian psychoanalysis may be the explanation for his own barbs at psychotherapists and existentialists.[1]

The names of neighbors and friends coming into the home of young Dietrich have the aura of greatness. Adolf von Harnack, the eminent historian of the church and of dogma, was both a neighbor and teacher. Ernst Troeltsch, the theologian and philosopher, was a frequent guest in the Bonhoeffer home. Other eminent people included Ferdinand Tönnies, and Max and Alfred Weber.

By age sixteen, Dietrich had decided to enter the ministry of the church. The decision gained little comment from his parents, but his brothers opposed it. His brother Klaus attempted to impress him with the purely provincial nature of the Protestant church in Germany and regretted that his brother should give his life to a superfluous cause. With resolution Dietrich replied, "If the Church is feeble, I shall reform it."[2] However facetious his reply might have been, it was portentous of the future way Bonhoeffer felt about the church's needs.

Karl Friedrich, another brother, talked with Dietrich about science and the universe it held up to behold, but at this point Dietrich would have nothing to do with science. When he could not argue against Karl Friedrich he simply commented, "You may knock my block off, but I shall still believe in God."[3] It was not until the years of his imprisonment that he seriously began to come to terms with science. This is one reason the *Letters and Papers* often sound so revolutionary.

Bonhoeffer began his study at Tübingen, but after a year moved to the University of Berlin in 1924. At Berlin, Bonhoeffer encountered a galaxy of erudite but often liberal scholars. Here Adolf Deissmann had made his contribution to New Testament studies. Hans Lietzmann was teaching the history of the early church, and Adolf von Harnack, Karl Holl, and Reinhold Seeberg were in one way or another connected with theology. Seeberg was the man under whom Bonhoeffer worked for the licentiate of theology, a degree comparable to the doctor of theology.

As a student, Bonhoeffer was precocious and independent. He did not simply absorb the liberalism of Berlin, nor did he become a true follower of the theologian Karl Barth, with whom he had many sympathies. Bonhoeffer did his homework well, and one of his fellow students described his performance:

> What really impressed me was not just the fact that he surpassed almost all of us in theological knowledge and capacity; but what passionately attracted me to Bonhoeffer was the perception that here was a man who did not only learn and gather in the *verba* and *scripta* of some master, but one who thought independently and already knew what he wanted and wanted what he knew. I had the experience (for me it was something alarming and magnificently new!) of hearing a young fair-haired student contradict the revered historian, his Excellency von Harnack, contradict him politely but clearly on positive theological grounds. Harnack answered, but the student contradicted again and again. I don't remember the content of the discussion—the talk was of Karl Barth—but I remember the secret enthusiasm that I felt for this free, critical and independent judgement in theology.[4]

In 1927, Bonhoeffer submitted his dissertation, *Sanctorum Communio: A Dogmatic Investigation of the Sociology of the Church*, to the faculty of the University of Berlin. This work was praised as a "theological miracle" by Karl Barth and was published three years later.

After his formal theological training at the university, Dietrich went to Barcelona, Spain, where he served in a position comparable to an assistant minister on an intern basis with a German-speaking congregation. His ability to relate to people of diverse conditions became apparent here in this congregation of small businessmen whose religious and cultural advancements had been small. As he worked with the elderly pastor and shared his life with the congregation, the church was resurrected in spirit and doubled in size. He started a service for children and a study group for boys in the sixth form (the last year) of their education. He gave pastoral care to the people and preached every two weeks. He became very attached to the people, and they returned the affection.

Upon his return to Berlin in 1929 Dietrich worked on his inaugural dissertation, a requisite for being permitted a faculty position in theology. In 1930, after completing *Act and Being: Transcendental Philosophy and Ontology in Systematic Theology,* he was given a position teaching systematic theology.

Before getting to the serious work of teaching, Bonhoeffer came to America for a year of study at Union Theological Seminary in New York City. His descriptions of religious life in America are revealing. He saw the students as less interested in real theology than in the practical element in Christianity. Their lack of interest in serious theology was partially expressed in their laughing out loud when a passage from Luther was quoted on sin and forgiveness. Yet Bonhoeffer noted the students' concern for the poor and needy, and he entered into their attempts to help relieve some of these problems. At Union also, he became aware of the growing problem of the Negro in America. He visited with Negroes in Harlem and attended a large Negro Baptist church for about six months.

Greatly unimpressed with American theology, he was more susceptible to its piety and social concern. Although Bonhoeffer impressed many American theologians with his own ability, he did not think too highly of the trend that theology was taking in America. A young Frenchman probably had more long-range influence on him than the American theologians. Jean Lasserre was an advocate of and a participant in the ecumenical movement. Moreover, he was a pacifist. Before meeting him, Bonhoeffer followed a traditional line of supporting a nationalistic attitude toward war and a critical attitude toward the ecumenical movement. In conversation Lasserre countered with: "Do we believe in the Holy Catholic Church, the Communion of the Saints, or do we believe in the eternal mission of France? One can't be a Christian and a nationalist at the same time."[5] Bonhoeffer later changed both his attitude toward pacifism—first accepting it and then modifying his view again—and his critical feelings toward the ecumenical movement.

By 1931, although he had enjoyed his stay in America, he was ready to return home and begin his period of lecturing at the University of Berlin. As a beginning lecturer, he had to depend upon his ability to attract students. They came out of curiosity at first. One student recalled, "He looked like a student himself when he went to the desk. But then our attention was so much riveted by what he had to say, that we no longer came for the sake of the very young man, but for the sake of his subject."[6] Except for the enjoyment of the students, Bonhoeffer led a rather lonely life in the unbending liberalism of the university. His independence of mind plus his affinity for Barth's theology made him suspect among the old-line theological liberals.

The year of his return to Germany brought momentous events in his life. In the summer of 1931 he journeyed to Bonn and met Karl Barth. His only regret was that he had not come sooner. A mutually respectful relationship grew through the years as indicated from the extant correspondence[7] and Barth's references in *Church Dogmatics* to Bonhoeffer's published works.[8] Barth's extremely critical letter about Bonhoeffer's later move to London could only have been written by a real friend.[9]

Also in this year, Bonhoeffer began an important relationship with the ecumenical movement. His flair for languages, theological precocity, and friendliness won him respect in the movement, and he was elected International Youth Secretary for Germany and Central Europe for the World Alliance of Churches. His involvement in the ecumenical work enabled him to convey to the free world the real status of Hitler's oppression of the church.

Meanwhile, in addition to his duties at the university which involved him in lecturing on systematic theology and leading a seminar on "The Idea of Philosophy and Protestant Theology," he became further involved in the ministry. He became student pastor at the Technical College in Berlin, and at the same time was requested to take over a confirmation class of fifty rowdy boys who lived in one of the roughest areas of Berlin. As the elderly pastor and young Dietrich ascended the stairs of the multi-storied building where the boys were, the children dropped rubbish on the two men below. At the top of the stairs the pastor tried to gain attention by shouting an introduction of Bonhoeffer. Some of the children only heard the word "Bon" and began to chant it, until the bewildered, frustrated old pastor left.

At first Dietrich stood in silence against the wall while the boys chanted. Then he began to speak softly to those near him. Out of curiosity the others began to be quiet. When the noise had subsided, he told them a story about Harlem and promised more next time if they behaved.[10] Not only did he win their attention for class instruction, but he moved into their neighborhood for two months to live among them. This most "hopeless" class was carried to its completion, and many of the boys remained long-time friends.

While busily engaged in the work of the university, Bonhoeffer continued to broaden his ecumenical contacts that would prove immensely helpful as the church situation became more crucial in the short years ahead. In 1932 he was very busy in his role as International Youth Secretary for Germany and Central Europe. He delivered an address, "The Church Is Dead," to the International Youth Conference meeting in Switzerland.[11] In the fall of 1932, he began a series of lectures which were later published as *Creation and Fall*.

The elections in Germany in 1932 brought about the Nazi rise to power, and the stage was set for the German church struggle. Bonhoeffer aligned himself with the evangelical opposition to Hitler. This alignment ultimately cost him his life.

In 1933 he gave a series of lectures on Christology which were never completed, nor published, except as they were reconstructed from the notes of students and published under the title *Christ the Center*. Following the summer session, Bonhoeffer took a leave of absence from the university and went to London to be minister of two German-speaking congregations. Although this move was opposed strenuously by Karl Barth, who looked upon Bonhoeffer's role in the church struggle as vital, the period served to strengthen his ties with the ecumenical movement, particularly with George Bell, Bishop of Chichester. During this interim period in London, Bonhoeffer attended the World Alliance of Churches meeting in Fanö, Denmark. Germany was represented only by the "German Christians," the pro-Hitler group. The council, due in part to Bonhoeffer's influence, denounced the "German Christians" and aligned its sympathies with the Confessing Church.

Through his growing world-wide friendships, Bonhoeffer received a letter of introduction to Gandhi and hoped to travel to India to study the methods of pacifism. These plans were interrupted by a call from the Confessing Church to come home and assume the leadership of an "illegal" seminary for training ministers. The call of duty won out over the desire to go to India, and he returned to a most dangerous task in Germany.

The seminary was eventually located at Finkenwalde, a tiny village south of Stettin on the Oder River in what was then Pomerania and is now Poland. There Bonhoeffer instituted a new type of theological education. He organized the students into a community with a "proper balance between work and worship, the academic and the practical, discipline and freedom."[12] The curriculum of the seminary provided for lectures by Bonhoeffer, reading of books, pastoral duties such as visitation, times of worship and confession of sin. Extracurricular community involvement included just plain fun, singing, doing dishes, and cleaning house. The experiences of the "brother-house" were recorded in *Gemeinsames Leben (Life Together)*, published in 1939.

As his work at the seminary progressed, Bonhoeffer attempted to retain his teaching post at the University of Berlin and did so until August 5, 1936, when it was withdrawn because of his opposition to Hitler's innovations in the church. His imperturbability was expressed in his comment, "I have long ceased to believe in the University."[13]

At Finkenwalde romance entered his life. Maria von Wedemeyer was seventeen years younger than he. Their first meeting was without meaning. She was only one among several grandchildren of Ruth von Kleist-Retzow, a well-to-do, spiritually minded widow who attended church at the seminary. Maria was to be included in the confirmation classes. Much later, after her graduation from high school she saw him again, and the rapport was spontaneous and immediate between them. Shortly after their engagement he was imprisoned. She saw him at least once a month in prison, and letters were exchanged as permission was allowed. Their engagement was a source of delight to him. Her visits formed a feeling of anticipation he treasured. He always wanted to know of her coming in advance, for without knowing he was cheated "out of the joy of anticipation and that is a very necessary part of your visit."[14]

During the troubled days of the late thirties, Bonhoeffer spoke a number of times on the subject of the "Visible and Invisible Church." The theme is one that had held his interest from his student days. He was very much concerned with the inner life, the question of communion, and the confession of the church. Bonhoeffer's ecumenical interest was not the kind that could overlook false doctrine as manifested in the German church. One of the weaknesses of the ecumenical movement, he wrote, was its lack of theology.[15]

Bonhoeffer's first popular work was published in 1937. As

a study of the Sermon on the Mount, *Nachfolge (The Cost of Discipleship)* harshly criticizes "cheap grace," which churches had been preaching, and calls for "costly" discipleship to Jesus Christ. In this same year the seminary was officially disbanded by the government, but it nevertheless maintained an underground existence until 1940.

Life was becoming more difficult for Bonhoeffer. He was faced with military service—a difficult thing for one who held pacifist views—but was needed by the Confessing Church for his leadership. Friends like Reinhold Niebuhr and Paul Lehmann tried to persuade him to come to America and were successful for a short time. Bonhoeffer was appointed to the faculty of the Union Theological Seminary for an indefinite period of time, and arrived in the United States on June 12, 1939. But the safety of America was too much for him, and he was back in Germany on July 25.

Bonhoeffer's diary records two different episodes during this brief period: "I do not understand why I am here. . . . The short prayer in which we thought of our German brothers almost overwhelmed me. . . . If things become more uncertain, I shall not stay in America. . . ." Later, after his decision to return home, he wrote, "Since I came on board ship, my mental turmoil about the future has gone."[16]

Back in Germany restrictions were placed on his movements. Berlin had been off-limits since 1938, although occasional visits were permitted. Now he was denied the right to speak anywhere in the Reich.

Bonhoeffer escaped military service by serving as a courier in the Intelligence Service, and thus was able to enjoy certain freedoms from the interference of the Gestapo. Certain members of the German Military Intelligence Service opposed Hitler, and eventually planned to assassinate him. Bonhoeffer came to accept the full implications of the resistance movement, justifying his position as follows: "It is not only my task to look after the victims of madmen who drive a motorcar in a crowded street, but to do all in my power to stop their driving at all." [17]

With an official pass, Bonhoeffer was able to travel outside Germany on behalf of the resistance movement without the Gestapo's awareness. In Geneva he talked with Visser't Hooft, General Secretary of the World Council of Churches, who asked him, "What do you pray for in these days?" Bonhoeffer replied, "If you want to know the truth, I pray for the defeat of my nation, for I believe that is the only way to pay for all the suffering which my country has caused in the world." [18]

Bonhoeffer was a liaison between the resistance movement and the free world, particularly Britain. He hoped that the Allied mandate of unconditional surrender might be changed if Hitler were overthrown and a new government formed, but the Allied forces proved adamant. Nevertheless, those in the Abwehr, the German Military Intelligence Service, went forward in their plans to eliminate Hitler. Bonhoeffer, forsaking his pacifist's views, agreed to cooperate but requested advance knowledge to enable him to sever ties with the Confessing Church. Not only would the Confessing Church not approve of the act, but it would mean the end of his career as a pastor.

Details of the plot against Hitler were worked out minutely for each person to have alibis for his actions. However, the rival spying arm of the Gestapo had been hoping to discredit leaders of the Abwehr on trumped up charges of bribery for helping Jews to escape Germany or, in the case of Bonhoeffer, of evading the draft. It was presumably on this charge that he was arrested on April 5, 1943. Two men arrived at his father's house in Berlin requesting to see Dietrich in his room. Without a search warrant or notice of arrest, Bonhoeffer was ordered to accompany them. He was taken to Tegel Military Prison in Berlin. At first conditions were extremely bad—the blankets, for instance, were too smelly to use. But after it was known who he was, his position improved.

Six months were to drag by before he was given a warrant for his arrest. The alibis of the plotters were all in order, and each played his part well. Bonhoeffer was able to have communication with the outside by means of coded messages passed in books and food parcels. Good-hearted guards made it possible for members of the family to visit and keep him informed.

Bonhoeffer spent eighteen months in Tegel Prison. Here he wrote the letters later incorporated into the intriguing work *Letters and Papers from Prison* (or as some editions title it, *Prisoner for God*). In passing the long hours of imprisonment, Bonhoeffer read the Bible and works ranging over such diverse subjects as literature, science, philosophy, theology, and history. Much of his reading related to the nineteenth-century cultural heritage of Germany.

In July 1944, another attempt on Hitler's life failed. Several had been made from various sources. The Gestapo's desire to incriminate the Abwehr was fulfilled in a dramatic way with the finding of the Abwehr's secret file in Zossen just two months later. The news spread quickly through the secret grapevine of the Abwehr, and Bonhoeffer heard it. Escape was the reaction to the news, and a plan had been made for some time. Arrangements were made with a friendly guard, and Bonhoeffer was to live "underground" until the destruction of Hitler came. Details were set in operation but halted when Dietrich's brother Klaus was arrested. The plan was jettisoned for fear that his family would be the scapegoats for his escape.

After the finding of the Zossen documents, Bonhoeffer was transferred to the Gestapo prison on Prinz-Albrecht-Strasse. Now along with others he was tortured to squeeze out information on collaborators. The evidence already on hand was enough to have them shot, but Hitler desired to ferret out all conspirators, and this desire prolonged their lives. Bonhoeffer remained on Prinz-Albrecht-Strasse until February

1945, when he was removed secretly to Buchenwald. On February 7, the guards assembled twenty of the most important prisoners and ordered them into two vehicles. Bonhoeffer was among them.

Payne Best, one of the survivors of Buchenwald, described Bonhoeffer during this time: "Bonhoeffer was different; just quite calm and normal, seemingly perfectly at his ease . . . his soul really shone in the dark desperation of our prison." [19] Bonhoeffer served as unofficial chaplain to many of the men of various nationalities. His spirit was gentle, and he became "the man for others" during the crucial days of Buchenwald. Best affirms, "He was one of the very few men I have ever met to whom God was real, and ever close to him." [20]

Hope and fear arose alternately in the hearts of the prisoners when Allied guns were heard on April 1, 1945. With the breakdown of the Nazi military system, hatred and vengeance yet ground on to the bitter end. On April 3, a lumbering enclosed vehicle pulled up to load sixteen prisoners including Bonhoeffer. Destination: Flossenbürg, an extermination camp in the Bavarian forest. The vehicle was turned away because the prison was full, and this raised the men's hopes temporarily. For a short time they were imprisoned in Schönberg, until two men appeared before the open door of Bonhoeffer's cell and called out: "Prisoner Bonhoeffer, get ready to come with us."

He moved quickly to place certain mementos in the hands of friends with instructions concerning them. He wrote his name in the beginning, middle, and end of a work by Plutarch —a book eventually returned to the Bonhoeffer family. He sent special greetings by Payne Best to his old friend, the Bishop of Chichester: "This is the end—for me the beginning of life."

At Flossenbürg, on April 8, a court martial met in full session. Dietrich was "tried" and sentenced to death—all in one night! The camp doctor of Flossenbürg recorded this impression of the events:

> On the morning of that day [April 9] between five and six o'clock the prisoners, among them Admiral Canaris, General Oster, General Thomas and *Reichgerichtsrat* Sack were taken from their cells, and the verdicts of the court martial read out to them. Through the half-open door in one room of the huts I saw Pastor Bonhoeffer, before taking off his prison garb, kneeling on the floor praying fervently to his God. I was most deeply moved by the way this lovable man prayed, so devout and so certain that God heard his prayer. At the place of execution, he again said a short prayer and then climbed the steps to the gallows, brave and composed. His death ensued after a few seconds. In the almost fifty years that I worked as a doctor, I have hardly ever seen a man die so entirely submissive to the will of God.[21]

Of these events, the family of Bonhoeffer knew nothing. A month later, Nazi Germany fell. Communication was difficult, and search was made for news of him. Geneva was the first to hear the news which was passed on to Bishop Bell. The elder Bonhoeffers were listening to the radio from London on July 27 when an English voice spoke: "We are gathered here in the presence of God to make thankful remembrance of the life and work of His servant Dietrich Bonhoeffer, who gave his life in faith and obedience to His holy word. . . ."[22]

With Bonhoeffer's death the church—and the world—was deprived both of a powerful intellect and of a creative Christian.

THE INTERPRETERS OF BONHOEFFER

How should one approach Bonhoeffer? This question must be raised because Bonhoeffer has become many things to many people as his influence continues to grow. He has been interpreted along thematic lines; i.e., his total work is viewed from the motif of Christology, ecclesiology, hermeneutics,[23] or some other theme. On the other hand, some interpreters use his later writings, particularly the *Letters and Papers from Prison*, as standard and ignore the earlier works to a large extent.

Our purpose in this work is to survey Bonhoeffer's work and thought. We are not defending any interpretation, but if this be forced upon us we would have to lean toward the "whole Bonhoeffer." Before embarking upon our survey, the reader can bear in mind that Bonhoeffer is viewed along several different lines. We offer the following sketch which is by no means exhaustive.

1. One of the early popularizers of Bonhoeffer was John A. T. Robinson, Bishop of Woolwich, who wrote *Honest to God*.[24] Bonhoeffer is an acknowledged mentor of Robinson, who draws freely on the *Letters and Papers from Prison*. Having read extracts of Bonhoeffer as early as 1952, he obtained the phrases, "God of the gaps," "world come of age," "man for others," and similar terms. But Robinson did not attempt an exposition of these phrases as other interpreters came to do. He attempted a method of correlation between Bonhoeffer and other writers, most often with Paul Tillich, the German-American theologian.

Robinson uses Bonhoeffer to raise what he terms pertinent questions, but with answers coming along Tillich's line of thought. This is unusual and a little strange, because Bonhoeffer's judgment was that the world passed Tillich by because he "sought to understand the world better than it understood itself."[25] In addition to Tillich, Robinson appeals to such diverse ideas as Rudolf Bultmann's demythologizing,[26] Julian Huxley's religion without revelation, and Albert Camus's understanding of man without God. These and other writers appear linked to Bonhoeffer either as saying the same thing he said in different words, or as providing answers to questions he raised.

One cannot help being suspicious of the link between Bonhoeffer and many of the writers that Robinson associates with him. The proposals they offered, particularly those of Tillich and Bultmann, were seriously questioned by Bonhoeffer. If this were not enough, one ought to be hesitant in using Bonhoeffer's incomplete, undeveloped, and enigmatic utterances.

2. Bonhoeffer is acclaimed as a major stimulus of the radical death-of-God movement. Paul M. Van Buren, often associated with this movement, uses Bonhoeffer as a springboard for setting forth his own brand of theology. He quotes the July 16, 1944, letter from prison for his platform, calling for a new theology without the God-hypothesis. Van Buren uses the services of linguistic analysis to repudiate any content-meaning for the word "God." In its place he builds his religious system upon the historical Jesus who, after the crucifixion, exercised a contagious influence on the disciples who perceived anew his unique brand of freedom.[27]

William Hamilton, another acknowledged leader of the movement, affirms Bonhoeffer's influence on his thought. While admitting that Bonhoeffer's meaning of "religionless Christianity" will probably remain unknown, Hamilton uses the term as a stimulus to set forth his own ideas. God as a problem-solver must be rejected, as well as the idea that man has a "God-shaped blank" within him.[28] Hamilton's brief sketch of Bonhoeffer on the twentieth anniversary of his death builds primarily on the *Letters*, showing that Bonhoeffer is important for the concepts of the "world coming of age" and "religionless Christianity."[29] The emphasis of Hamilton and others in the related *Honest to God Debate* has caused some critics to misread Bonhoeffer and accuse him of practical atheism.[30]

The implication of atheism is not the usual story of the interpreters of Bonhoeffer, however. David Jenkins, in his

Guide to the Debate About God, cautions, "Whatever Bonhoeffer meant by his call to Christians to be 'without religion' it is clear that· it was no call to be 'without God'."[31] Bonhoeffer criticizes religion but "presupposes the existence of the Christian fellowship and the givenness of the Bible."[32]

3. The literature on Bonhoeffer in Germany is divided into two schools. The position of Gerhard Ebeling centers on the hermeneutical implications of the *Letters and Papers from Prison.* The other group considers the "whole Bonhoeffer" and uses a motif study generally along Christological lines. This is the view of Eberhard Bethge,[33] the close friend of Bonhoeffer. Jürgen Moltmann follows this position in his essay, "The Lordship of Christ and Human Society,"[34] in which he analyzes the *Letters* in light of the "complete" Bonhoeffer. Along a similar line is Jürgen Weissbach's essay, "Christology and Ethics."[35]

4. In America one of the early important works was that of John Godsey, *The Theology of Dietrich Bonhoeffer.*[36] Godsey treats Bonhoeffer's theology from the standpoint of Christ existing as the church, that is, using ecclesiology[37] as the clue to his thought. Questions have been raised about Godsey's method of fitting the later works into this framework when they do not seem to deal with ecclesiology per se. Yet in spite of criticism of this motif by some writers,[38] a noteworthy work by a Roman Catholic follows this ecclesiological motif. William Kuhns, who is the first Roman Catholic to write a book on Bonhoeffer, stands in substantial agreement with the view of Godsey.[39]

John A. Phillips criticizes Godsey and himself writes of Bonhoeffer from the standpoint of Christology, asserting that Jesus Christ is "the best clue to his thinking."[40] Although Bonhoeffer's Christology developed, Phillips maintained that it is a constant motif throughout his writings. Even in the light of Phillips's criticism of Godsey, it may be questioned whether a real distinction can be made between ecclesiology and the doctrine of Christ in Bonhoeffer.

One other work may be noted in this brief survey. William B. Gould uses discipleship as the basic organizing theme in his work, *The Worldly Christian*.[41] While it is an interesting organizational device, it is doubtful if discipleship means anything without the Christological perspective. There are other interesting and useful works, but we now turn to Bonhoeffer himself.

II. The Shape of the Church

Bonhoeffer's first and in many ways most difficult work was the *Sanctorum Communio*, or using the English title, *The Communion of Saints*.[1] It is abstract, technical, and important. That it did not command a wide reading audience is understandable. This work is not an example of the "popular" Bonhoeffer. Yet there is justification for beginning with it because Bonhoeffer was vitally concerned with the church for most of his short life. The book serves as the foundation for much of his writings, and we want to build upon it. Should the reader bog down here, he might with justification turn to chapter IV and continue there to the end of this work before coming back to chapter II.[2]

DEFINING SOCIOLOGY AND THE CHURCH

The Communion of Saints attempts to relate sociology and theology to one another. Sociology is defined as "the science of the structures of empirical communities."[3] An empirical community is one that can be viewed objectively. Bonhoeffer aimed then to study the church from the standpoint of sociology. If, however, one is to understand a religious community, one must examine it from within, taking the claims of the community seriously. Without assuming this internal stance, the church cannot be understood at all.

Because the religious community is composed of people, it becomes necessary to define the Christian concept of person. The concept of person will determine the type of community that will come forth. Bonhoeffer speaks of different types: Aristotelian (man becomes a person by partaking of reason); Stoic ("a man becomes a person by submitting to a higher obligation");[4] Epicurean (man's life is heightened by pleasure, though it has a "defective concept of spirit");[5] and the idealist tradition flowing from Immanuel Kant (the perceiving person is the starting point for philosophy).

Bonhoeffer trades blows predominantly with the idealist tradition. In turn, he defines the Christian concept of a person in nonstatic terms. Person is fluctuating and can be said to exist only "when a man is morally responsible."[6] The person comes into existence only when "he is passionately involved in a moral struggle, and confronted by a claim which overwhelms him."[7] Into this struggle Bonhoeffer introduces the idea of a "barrier" that man faces. The barrier involves "the absolute distinction between God and man."[8] The deeper man realizes this separation to be, the more profound will his self-understanding be. The barrier is a problem for man not only with reference to God, but with other men in community. In community the "I" is confronted by a "Thou" which may be either God or man. Yet one may not know oneself as a "Thou," nor can one know another person as an "I."

Bonhoeffer rejects the idea that encounter creates persons, and declares that "God, or the Holy Spirit, comes to the concrete Thou, only by his action does the other become a Thou for me, from which my I arises. In other words, every human Thou is an image of the divine Thou."[9] Thus Bonhoeffer concludes that personhood is related to social relations.

Building upon his definition of person, Bonhoeffer develops the idea with reference to man's first state of existence before God in contrast to man's existence after rebellion against God. In contrast to idealism, which knows only con-

tinuity in man's life in the Spirit, Bonhoeffer recognizes sin
as a reality in history. The conflict of man with God poses
problems for any idea of community, but community is God's
design for man. Thus ethics and morality have meaning only
in sociality.

If man stands in community, what is the relation of the
community to his own being? Bonhoeffer answers: "The individual personal spirit lives solely by virtue of sociality, and
the 'social spirit' becomes real only in individual embodi-
ment." [10] Therefore Bonhoeffer can speak of both the individual and a collective being. [11] The design of God for men to
live in community leads to the natural question of the religious community.

The community is constituted by desire, or will, and not
necessarily on the idea of commonness, or formal agreement.
Because willing is important, conflict thereby arises in the
community. Bonhoeffer assesses several forms of human relationships: the community, the society, and the mass. A community is where "life is lived," a society is an association in
rational action, and the mass is man caught up by stimuli in
which there are no real social bonds. [12] The idea of the community—the willed entity—is important for the form of the
church. [13]

Having set forth his idea of community, Bonhoeffer relates
it to sin's entry which causes a broken community. Sin breaks
communion with God and man, and man with man. The
natural forms of community are now corrupted. Why is the
phenomena of sin universal? In answer he says that the Bible
speaks of the universality of sin but nothing of original sin.
Bonhoeffer's solution is that "the guilt of the individual and
the universality of sin should be conceived of together." [14]
Sin must not be understood biologically. Instead, sin and guilt
are the bases for understanding the species, or mankind. The
race is in sin because I am in sin. With each individual falling
into sin, the race falls, and hence "in principle none of us is

distinct from Adam—which also means, however, that each of us is the 'first' sinner."[15] Sin itself is unfathomable. One might understand it psychologically up to the deed, but "the deed itself is . . . psychologically inexplicable."[16]

Building upon the idea that sin affects the species, Bonhoeffer proceeds to speak of collective persons. Israel is an example of God's relation to the collective group. "It was the people, and not the individuals, who had sinned."[17] A community—the collective person—stands before God and is dealt with as a whole regardless of what certain individuals may or may not do. The old race in Adam is a collective person in contrast to the new collective person, "Christ existing as the church."[18] Yet a collective person is subject to fragmentation.

WHAT THE CHURCH IS

The heart of the book comes in a long chapter (118 pages) entitled "Sanctorum Communio." In setting forth basic principles, Bonhoeffer declares that "the Christian concept of the church is reached only by way of the concept of revelation."[19] He rejects as untenable the explanation that a concept of "the Holy" leads to community.[20] Accepting the revelatory nature of the church, he briefly sketches the New Testament view of the church. The significance of this lies in the conviction that equates the two statements "to be in Christ" and "to be in the church."[21] This equation means that "Christ is really present only in the church."[22] Bonhoeffer does not mean that a second incarnation takes place but that "we must think of a revelatory form in which 'Christ exists as the church.' "[23] The church so understood brings together many persons, is a community, and has unity, although it is not without conflict of wills.

Regardless of sin and man's alienation in the primal state, God's purpose for man is in the church.[24] The isolation of

man from man and from God is nullified in the life and
death of Christ. Repentance becomes the avenue of entry into
the new community and the exit out of the community of
Adam. The new community is unlike other communities in
that the Holy Spirit lives in it.

There are other implications of the central theme: the
church is Christ and Christ is the church. Christ in the church
is related to the Word through which the Spirit speaks. Christ
is in the Word and the Word is directed to "a plurality of
hearers." [25] The Spirit is active in three sociological relationships: the individual spirit of man, the spiritual community,
and spiritual oneness. The Spirit makes a claim on the individual in his loneliness, to bring him to Christ. In trusting
Christ, men are made members of the divine community.
Being a new creation, they come to know the meaning of
agape. Love seeking a response means communion with God
and man. Loving communion also means self-surrender to
the "Thou" before man—either God or man.

The acts of love for man in community with Christ are:
(1) self-renunciation—to work for others by giving up personal claims to happiness; (2) intercessory prayer; and (3)
"the mutual granting of forgiveness of sins in God's name." [26]
Bonhoeffer's comments on intercessory prayer follow the inspiration of Luther and need serious reconsideration in
modern times. More controversial is the matter of mutual
granting of forgiveness. This leads most naturally to Bonhoeffer's proposal that a Protestant confession be reinstituted,
but only if proper instruction is given concerning its meaning.

Bonhoeffer's treatment of spiritual oneness anticipates a
theology for the ecumenical movement. Spiritual unity is
willed by God and is not the result of a concord or agreement
between men. Unity is misunderstood. The unity of the New
Testament is not "one theology and one rite, one opinion
upon all things both public and private, and one mode of
conduct in life," but rather "one body and one Spirit, one

Lord, one faith, one baptism. . . ." [27] Oneness and unity are
different. Oneness suggests conformity; unity exhibits the
possibility of diversity in the Spirit. This unity is invisible,
but it must be believed.[28] On the ecumenical movement, Bonhoeffer declares that "unification from below is not the same
as unity from above." The first may never be achieved, but
the second is real. Spiritual unity is related to equality. There
is equality before God, but neither in the church nor in any
community are men identical.

He devotes considerable space to the empirical form of
the church. The church is simultaneously the community of
the holy as well as a community of sinners. The church is not
to be identified with the kingdom of God; rather, it is the
kingdom of Christ and does not include Old Testament believers. He rejects the "gathered-church" concept for the
Lutheran *Volkskirche* or national-church concept.[29] The universal church embraces "all individual churches." [30]

The church has certain functions, primarily worshiping.
There is need of a ministry to a congregation, for preaching
is divinely ordained. The function, not the person, is ordained
to the congregation. For a Christian to be unattached to a
congregation is "unthinkable" as a reality.[31] The church also
comes together for the sacraments. Bonhoeffer follows a
Lutheran position on infant baptism, in which faith is located
by proxy in the congregation rather than the infant. Because
Bonhoeffer takes the church seriously as life in Christ, he
looks critically at the pietistic movements designated as "the
church within the church." [32] Movements on this order lead
to factions and peril.

His treatment shows deep respect for the church, and he
argues that it has authority because it rests upon the Word.[33]
This may produce a threat to the freedom of the conscience,
but obedience is due to the church, and it occasionally may
need to demand the sacrifice of the intellect. Rebellion
against the church by the individual member is a serious

matter for God alone to decide; "the only valid motive . . . would be a perfect obedience rooted in the closest attachment to the church and to the Word in it." [34]

Toward the end of this work, Bonhoeffer discusses the church as an independent sociological type. It is not an association which can be banded and disbanded by agreement. It is not an institution, in the sense held by Max Weber and Ernst Troeltsch, where grace and gifts are dispensed to the dues-paying members. Even the term community is not fully adequate, for although it has affinities to the community, the church is one of a kind.[35] The uniqueness of the community is found in its divine institution rather than in pure doctrine.

Growing out of his rejection of "the purity" of doctrine [36] as a norm for the church, Bonhoeffer admits that the state or "national" church and the "gathered" church belong together. The national church stands in peril if it is not reaching out. In a brief section on the church and the proletariat, he discusses the inwardness of the national church. The church cannot be satisfied with a middle-class norm but must reach the working man in his language and culture. The future church will change from its bourgeois form to what? Bonhoeffer did not profess to know, but he was sure it would change.[37]

The last word on the church is an eschatological [38] one. The church will be redeemed collectively and individually. On how the collective feature will take place Bonhoeffer admits ignorance, but yet affirms its truth. The future community of God will involve the resurrection of the body, "a new corporality for the godless as well." [39] Intrigued by the possibility of universal salvation for all mankind, he yet rejects it as a part of his system. The end of the story of the church is its incorporation into "the kingdom of God in all the world." [40]

By way of a brief assessment, the following may be offered. First, sociologists will fail to see an empirical treatment of the church, but instead will find a highly abstract theological approach to it. Second, to the "free" church tradition it will appear that Bonhoeffer saw the church more from the Lutheran national-church pattern rather than taking seriously the New Testament forms. The national-church form seeks to justify some practices that seem contrary to certain concepts of Christian faith. For instance, faith appears incompatible with infant baptism, and the national church appears contrary to personal commitment and choice. Bonhoeffer follows the attitude of Luther concerning the so-called "radicals" who advocated a gathered church, and adult or believers' baptism based upon personal commitment in faith.

At the same time, it must be said that this work is a significant study in the nature of the church because the position is maintained that the church is not just another organization, it is the Body of Christ. Bonhoeffer's treatment of this question is relevant today, since the church is puzzling over its own nature, its role, its renewal. Does the church have political, economic, and other social responsibilities? For Bonhoeffer, the church is unique. If it will not be the church, the Body of Christ, its existence cannot be defended. This truth must be maintained as well as regained where it has been lost.

III. The Church:
Objective Source of Revelation

Bonhoeffer's second work, *Act and Being*, was written in 1931 and presented as his inaugural dissertation, giving him the right to lecture at the university. *Act and Being*, like the first work, is abstract and difficult to read. Certainly Bonhoeffer's popularity has come from other works than these. Yet *Act and Being* deals with the important problem of revelation. What philosophical modes should be used to express God's self-revelation? Should one speak only of God's self-revelation as events in biblical history? Is there a better way of speaking of God's self-revelation than in the category of being? Is there some other alternative? Bonhoeffer treats these questions in three parts in his work.

THE ALTERNATIVES OF PHILOSOPHY

Part One exposes the problem of act and being as a problem of how and what one may know, especially about God. He treats two alternatives: the transcendental and the ontological endeavors. The transcendental approach is traced from Immanuel Kant to Karl Barth who, at the time, was regarded by Bonhoeffer as being dependent upon Kant in some ways. The development of philosophical thought from Kant (1724–1804) to G. W. F. Hegel (1770–1831) serves as a backdrop to these issues. In his theory of knowledge, Kant divided reality into two types: phenomena and noumena. We experience phenomena only by the senses in the things we see, hear, taste, touch, etc. The noumena, or the reality behind appearances, the thing-in-itself, can never be known by the senses, and hence cannot be known at all. Noumena may refer to God or the existence of the soul. Bonhoeffer is especially interested in the subject of God, for he is transcendent. How is one to know God, the numinous? Needless to say, Bonhoeffer introduces the idea of God's self-revelation, in which God comes to man who is incapable of searching out God on his own. But in what way and how is this done? This is a crucial question for Bonhoeffer, and to this we will return later.

Kant's successors eliminated the distinction between phenomena and noumena. In Kant there was always something set over against the personal "I" which was not known. In later philosophers when the noumena was dropped, God and the self became identified.[1] There are serious problems both with Kant's transcendental philosophy and with the idealism of his "specious" successors. Bonhoeffer's main criticisms are directed at Kant's successors. If the "I" becomes paramount, its knowledge is restricted. It never knows anything other than itself. Thus, what is supposed to be revelation is turned into the study of anthropology or psychology. God "becomes the prisoner of the consciousness." [2] "What reason can learn from itself (thus Hegel) is revelation, and so God is incarcerated in consciousness." [3] Equally untenable is the inference that "if God is to come to man, man must be in essence divine." [4] Bonhoeffer admits that transcendentalism has a solution, but that it is inadequate without "radical transformation and completion." [5]

The second alternative is the ontological endeavor. A true ontology,[6] says Bonhoeffer, aims at showing real being existing apart from consciousness. "Systematic ontology supposes pure being to be intuitively beheld in its transcendence of consciousness." [7] In his treatment Bonhoeffer outlines the approach of Edmund Husserl (1859–1938), the father of philosophical phenomenology. Phenomenology "is the study of the phenomena in the pure consciousness." [8] Husserl rejected the Kantian concept of noumena, and this led him to affirm greater areas of knowledge for man. More than simply knowing phenomena, one might know being.[9] Because Husserl says that man can intellectually intuit being, Bonhoeffer places him in the idealist tradition. But as far as the question of God is concerned, Husserl attains no great clarity and does not advance beyond the purely human word of Hegel. He may shed light on man's way of thinking but not on the problem of being.

In this alternative Bonhoeffer treats the view of Max Scheler (1874–1928) who altered Husserl's emphases somewhat but who, for Bonhoeffer, did not solve anything. Also included is a pupil of Husserl, Martin Heidegger (b. 1889). For Heidegger, being is "understood from Dasein" or existence. Existence is known by an existential analysis of man. Although Heidegger aims at exposing being to the philosophical world, he never proceeds further than man. The implication, for Bonhoeffer, is that Heidegger has left no room for the idea of revelation [10] and is useless for purposes of theology.

The last example of a being-approach to theology is that of Roman Catholic writers. Up to this point the transcendence of God has been either rejected, overlooked, or identified with nature. In Thomism, God's transcendence is allowed. Thomism, which follows the principles elaborated by St. Thomas Aquinas (1225–1274), employs the *analogia entis* or analogy of being. The analogy of being supposes that God has left a trace of himself in nature which indirectly and proportionately testifies of himself. Thomism rejects the identification of God and man, yet argues that some likeness of God is perceived in man. But if one accepts the *analogia* as useful for theology, one may arrive at a "being" which may not be God.[11] Being is still self-projection, and thus is not successful.

The offending element in all these attempts at arriving at being is that they suppose that man is capable of bestowing truth on himself. One fundamental problem in this issue is man and his sin. Bonhoeffer declares, "Thought is as little able as good works to deliver the *cor curvum in se* from itself."[12] There is little room for revelation in philosophy. Philosophy's hope is to confess itself as Christian, for it seeks to give, and cannot, what only Christ can give in understanding the universe and man.[13]

THE PROBLEM STATED FOR THEOLOGY

Part Two deals with the act-being problem in revelation. Revelation is defined in terms of the acts of God. Thus revelation is transcendent. When God comes to man this act becomes the means whereby man can know the truth of God and come to understand himself. Revelation as act means: (1) that God is free; (2) that man is receptive; (3) that God is not "haveable" or graspable, in the sense that he comes under man's power through knowledge; (4) that God is known only because of self-revealing grace. Consequently, God is nonobjective and nonavailable. In act, "God is always the 'coming', not the 'existing' deity (Barth)."[14] If God is conceived in act as nonobjective, Bonhoeffer concludes that one may also speak of faith as nonobjective. The practical problem of the act-theology relates to decision. Is not the act inadequate in fulfilling the needs of the "everydayness" of the religious life and decision?[15] The religious life needs some basis for continuity.

The alternative to the above position is to speak of revelation in terms of being, and this can take one of three possibilities: (1) doctrine, (2) psychic experience, and (3) an institutional form.[16] The latter may be understood as the institution of the Catholic Church or the Protestant idea of verbal inspiration of the Bible. Bonhoeffer rejects all three of these because

> they understand the revealed God as an entity, whereas entities are transcended by act and being. Man assimilates them into his transcendental I, and so they are unable to be objective in the full sense, hence are useless for theological explanation of the revelation in Christ. . . .[17]

While any of these may be reassuring, man is always in control of them.

A true and meaningful ontology, or being theology, "must satisfy two all-important requirements: 1. it must involve the existence of man; 2. it must be possible to think of the being in continuity," i.e., it must define "being in." [18] Because these two alternatives, revelation as act and revelation as being, are inadequate *alone*, Bonhoeffer turns to a synthesis in which act and being take on a new dimension in the church.

BONHOEFFER'S SOLUTION

The heart of his proposal is in the chapter, "The Church as a Unity of Act and Being." Assuming the inadequacy of philosophy's understanding of existence, Bonhoeffer declares that existence can be understood only in the church, because the church gives an explanation "outside" of man. Revelation is only confronted in the church. Thus revelation is not the past remembered, but exists presently and continually in the church, for "the Church is the Christ of the present, 'Christ existing as community'. . . . Christ is the corporate person of the Christian communion." [19]

Because of the personal involvement of Christ in the church, Bonhoeffer asserts that the old issue of act *or* being, as it relates to revelation, is now resolved. God gives himself in act to the individual who at the same time is in the communion of Christ. Man's existence is affected because he is "in Christ." If man's existence were unchanged, being in the community of revelation "would be pointless." [20]

Bonhoeffer claims that the problem of subjectivism is overcome because the church is "concretely visible." [21] Faith supposes an object outside of itself, but faith is a mode of being in the church. Although faith might be viewed as a series of broken discrete acts, Bonhoeffer declares that "faith as an act knows itself as the mode of being of its being in the church, the continuity is indeed only 'in the believing' but thereby is really preserved as being in the Church." [22] Even sin does not disrupt the continuity of the new existence of man in Christ. Man's inability to put himself beyond "the pale of God's commonwealth" underlines the "everydayness" of life in the church—which is in Christ. [23]

Bonhoeffer closes [24] his work by considering the act-being problem in man. Man has a relationship to either Adam or Christ. In either case, revelation is necessary to know this. [25] The act-being relation for "being in Adam" is the problem of sin. Sin must be defined initially as a willful "act." But if sin were only an act, "it would be theoretically and humanly possible to find one's way back to a sinless being." [26] The death of Christ would have been unnecessary. Bonhoeffer does not assume a historical beginning point of sin with Adam. Rather viewing man as a corporate being, he declared, "I myself am Adam, am I and humanity together; in me falls humanity; as I am Adam, so is every individual, but then in all individuals the one person of humanity, Adam, is active." [27] Thus the "everydayness of Adam" is related to the "everydayness" of life—man's sin is both act and being. In act he is responsible, in being he corrupts the rest of mankind. Being in Adam means guilt, despair, isolation, temptation, and death. [28] Being in Christ is to become a new being, yet one susceptible to the old being's influence. But faith brings forgiveness for guilt, hope for despair, communion with God instead of isolation, help for temptation, and life through death.[29] The new being belongs to the future; the old being belongs to the past.

In closing this chapter, certain questions may be raised about Bonhoeffer's ideas. First the concreteness of the church and its objectivity are points quite well taken, but one wonders whether Bonhoeffer fully distinguishes his view from the Roman Catholic view of the church, particularly when Roman Catholicism sees the church as the mystical body of Christ. Second, his emphasis on faith as a gift of God, rather than salvation being a gift of God (Eph. 2:8), is suspect exegetically. When faith is regarded as a gift of God, faith as response and commitment is sidetracked. This is particularly pertinent to the issue of infant baptism.[30] Third, one feels uneasy and unclear about Bonhoeffer's use of the term "God's Word." It is used with ambiguity because he speaks decisively about God's Word but then rejects the role of Scripture as incapable of fulfilling the demands of the "being" aspect of revelation. The Bible becomes an "entity," "whereas entities are transcended by act and being."[31] This is particularly puzzling since one of Bonhoeffer's favorite passages of Scripture is Isaiah 55:11 in which God promises that his Word would not return to him without fulfilling his purposes. Since the Word of God is described as a double-edged sword which man cannot control, Bonhoeffer's view seems out of character with his overall position.

IV. The Church
Seeking to Know Itself

We turn now to Bonhoeffer's work, *Christ, the Center*. The choice is an arbitrary one, but perhaps not without justification. The lectures entitled *Creation and Fall* could well be considered next, because the questions raised in *Creation and Fall* brought Bonhoeffer to consider the place of Christ.

Christology is fundamental to Bonhoeffer's thought, yet in turning to the Christology we have an unusual problem. The Christology lectures are reconstructions of notes taken by students. Eberhard Bethge, the man who knows Bonhoeffer most intimately, reconstructed them, and their accuracy is enhanced by his position and understanding of Bonhoeffer. The lectures were delivered in the summer semester of 1933 at the University of Berlin. Intended to be complete in three parts, Bonhoeffer only finished two of them.

QUESTIONS ABOUT CHRIST

The introduction places the question of Christology in its setting. Christology must be studied by the worshiping community. The Word of God, the Logos, is not an idea which cannot be worshiped, but a person. How does one understand a person? The meaningful question is: *Who* are you? The wrong questions are: *What* are you? or *How* can you be what you are?

Bonhoeffer rejects two questions in Christology. The first is: How should the Incarnation be conceived? The early church foundered on this one. The second is: What is this being? Modern liberal theology foundered on this question. The New Testament and, of course, Bonhoeffer's inspiration, Luther, followed the middle path. The central question is: Who is this Person?

Bonhoeffer questions the traditional rubric of theology, "the person and work of Christ." [1] The question was asked: "Does the work interpret the person or the person the work?" Bonhoeffer agrees with Luther that the person determines the meaning of the work, not the other way around. The work may appear good, but it could have been done by the devil. If the person is primary, then an "example-type" religion is out, because Jesus is the Son of God. A merely idealistic founder can be imitated, but the Son of God does a work which I am not capable of imitating. All avenues to God are excluded through the self-revelation in Christ wherein is learned his work. "If I know *who* the person is who does this, I will also know *what* he does." But the separation of person and work is artificial. We have to do with the "whole Christ, the one Christ . . . . [who] is the historical *(geschictliche)* Jesus. . . ." [2]

Christ, the Center is divided into two parts. The first is "The Present Christ—The 'Pro Me'." It emphasizes the contemporaneity of Christ and what he is for me. Two theological statements serve as the basis of Bonhoeffer's views. First, "Jesus is the Christ present as the Crucified and Risen One." Second, "Christ is present in the church as a person." [3] In clarifying his position Bonhoeffer rejects any understanding of Christ as an influence, a force, or anything short of being a person. Further, Christ must not be viewed as something outside history. Rather, Christ is a historical person who, because of the resurrection, still confronts men in history on a personal basis. Perhaps a third statement summarizes his position on Christology: Jesus Christ is all of this—*for me*.

Granting these assertions, Christ is said to confront men in three ways. (1) In the Word. The Word is not met as an idea, which is abstract and timeless, but as person. An idea demands no commitment, but a person-to-person communication demands a response. In being confronted with the Word, man is "put in the truth." Thus Christ does not declare a way to God, but *is* the way. Ideas are held by man, but the Logos holds man.[4]

(2) In the sacrament. Bonhoeffer presents a Lutheran view of Christ as sacrament. "The Word in the sacrament is an embodied Word." Not all of nature is a sacrament, only the creaturely elements which "God addresses, names and hallows with his special Word," that is, with Jesus Christ. "This Word Jesus Christ is wholly present in the sacrament, not only his Godhead, and not only his manhood."[5] Symbolic interpretations of the sacrament are rejected: the sacraments "do not *mean* something, they *are* something."[6]

Bonhoeffer attempts to resolve the differences between Lutherans and Calvinists by denying the validity of the questions they raised. The "how" of the sacrament brought up the Calvinist question of how Christ's bodily limitations in heaven could be present in the sacrament. The Lutherans answered with their communication of attributes of the divine nature, or the doctrine of the ubiquity of his flesh. This question is rejected. One may only ask, "*Who* is present in the sacrament?" The answer is: "The whole person of the God-man is present in his exaltation and his humiliation; Christ exists in such a way that he is existentially present in the sacrament."[7]

(3) In the community. Christ as community speaks of the presence of Christ in the church. This means "that the Logos of God has extension in space and time in and as the community."[8] "The Word is *in* the community in so far as the community is a recipient of revelation."[9] To say that the community is the Body of Christ is not a metaphor, it *is* his body.

The contemporaneity of Christ is viewed from three perspectives: (1) Christ is the center of human existence. Although this cannot be demonstrated, the center of Christ is seen where man fails to fulfill the law and Christ is the fulfillment of it for man. (2) Christ is the center of history. Man's history holds forth promise and fulfillment. The promise of history, being corrupted by sin, has experienced only corrupt messiahs, apart from that one in Israel in whom God fulfilled his promise.[10] Like the first, this is proclaimed, not demonstrated. (3) Christ is "the Mediator between God and Nature."[11] Nature, not being free and thereby not having guilt, cannot be reconciled, only redeemed. The sacrament, speaking of an old thing become a new creature, proclaims a word for nature. Christ is the liberator of creation.[12]

WRONG ANSWERS ABOUT CHRIST

In the second half of his work, Bonhoeffer speaks of the history of doctrines concerning Christ. The familiar distinction made by modern liberalism—the historical Jesus versus the Christ of faith—is rejected by Bonhoeffer. There is only one historical Jesus Christ.[13] In this Bonhoeffer follows the conclusions of Martin Kähler.[14] The Logos, who is personal, who is incarnate in Jesus of Nazareth, is confronted through the historical scriptural narratives and is known in no other way or form.

The history of Christology shows that the wrong questions have been asked: *how* rather than *who?* Bonhoeffer deals with the early heresies of doceticism, Ebionism, monophysitism, Nestorianism,[15] and others, and concludes that the Council of Chalcedon in A.D. 451 rightly condemned these early attempts to deal with an invalid question. He rejects the charge that Chalcedon was a compromise solution. Actually it safeguarded the real question: Who is incarnate in Jesus Christ?

Chalcedon's conclusion gave impetus to theological development in Protestantism. Much of the development followed the "how" pattern. How can one relate the power of God to the powerlessness of man? How can God be tired, hungry, and thirsty? These questions cropped up in the Reformation. Luther gave the answer of the *communicatio idiomatum,* or the interpenetration of attributes of each nature.[16] On the basis of the *communicatio idiomatum,* the Lutherans could say that the body of Jesus Christ is omnipresent and thereby affirm a real presence in the sacraments.

The Calvinistic tradition dissented by saying that Lutheran Christology is no longer talking about the Savior of the New Testament. The Lutheran view says that a change in God takes place, and that the real humanity of Christ is illusory.[17] The human nature of Christ is taken up in the attributes of deity. Thereby Luther could be charged with reviving the ancient heresy of monophysitism.

The solutions of post-Lutheran orthodoxy developed a Christology around the humiliations of Christ. Two types arose: the Kenoticists, who spoke of Christ renouncing the use of his divine nature, and the Cryptics, who spoke of the powers of deity being concealed during the Incarnation. Bonhoeffer rejected these because neither the divinity nor the humanity of Jesus were made comprehensible. The touchstone for his Christology is Chalcedon. To this he returns repeatedly.

Although a section on the "Eternal Christ" was proposed, it was never completed, or did not survive. We can make some evaluations on what remains of his lectures. Very significant is the question of *who,* rather than *how,* in the Incarnation. The merit of establishing different ground rules in the Christological discussion is noteworthy. The avoidance of speculative questions which cannot be answered would have saved the early church much heartache. Bonhoeffer does appear arbitrary in some of his positions, however. A question in passing relates to his attitude toward "the hypothesis of the Virgin Birth." [18] He regards the biblical evidence for it as indecisive and uncertain. One can justly wonder what hermeneutical principle Bonhoeffer employs to determine for himself that certain things are "biblical" and others are "not biblical." He accepts the miracles of Jesus as being genuine, although performed incognito. This appears to be an arbitrary distinction.

In another example he describes the sacrament as a stumbling block. In his attempt to rid Christianity of "religious elements" is arbitrariness not at work? Is not Bonhoeffer subject to the same criticism as many theologians? I may jettison as "religion" those items which are scandals to me, while those items I keep are the essential nature of Christianity. But in reality, what I keep may be a binding tradition which someone else is eager to cut out as being a "burden" to modern man. Is not the real scandal or stumbling block the fact that I choose to make it that? Is not the whole ecumenical movement stopped here? What is a scandal—verbal inspiration, for instance—to one may be the very nature of authority to another. In spite of these criticisms, *Christ, the Center* is a fruitful book for its emphasis on religious knowledge. If God is not incarnate in Jesus Christ, we have no knowledge of him that is worth knowing.

LECTURES ON GENESIS

In the winter semester of 1932–33, Bonhoeffer gave a series of lectures on the first three chapters of Genesis. They were well received by his students, who persuaded him to publish them. They appeared in 1937 under the title *Schöpfung und Fall (Creation and Fall)*.[19] The lectures present a theological rather than exegetical exposition of the Genesis chapters. Bonhoeffer's interest in Christo-ecclesiology still prevails in these lectures. Particular attention is directed toward the Bible as the book of the church.

The chapters reflect the outline of Genesis. The beginning is treated not as a point in time which man cannot know, but

is referred to the One who was there—God. It is impossible
to search behind God's creative act. Creation is a free act
without cause or necessity. The God who creates is linked by
Bonhoeffer to the God of the resurrection. No Marcionite [20]
gnosticism is permitted. The resurrection of Christ is essentially a creation out of nothing and by it we know of the
original creation. God the beginning is at the same time the
end of man.

God the Creator stands *over* the waters in creation. No ancient cosmogonic identification of God and the world is permitted. God gives it form and direction, but he himself is
glorified in the creation. In fact, Bonhoeffer declares that
"God is worshipped first by the earth," [21] which might raise
questions about worship as an act of free creatures toward a
Creator.

God creates by his Word. Speaking is akin to freedom. Because God works in the world as transcendent, we know him
only by means of the Word. The ways of knowing God by
natural theology (eminence, negation, and causality) are
rejected because of the revelatory Word.[22] Indeed, it is not
true to speak of the creation as an "effect" of the Creator. To
reason from effect to cause means that God "had" to create.
More correctly God created in freedom without necessity. The
world God created is "good," but this does not mean that this
is the best of all possible worlds. Its goodness "consists in its
being under the dominion of God." [23] God continues to uphold
the creation (the doctrine of preservation).

In writing of the second day of creation, Bonhoeffer rejects
its "ancient world picture in all its scientific *naïveté*." [24] The
question arises as to why he should be so rigid in his rejection
of this account, when earlier the point is labored that we cannot know anything of the beginnings.[25] In spite of this problem, he introduces the concept of fixedness in which the laws
of days, years, and seasons are understood.

With the appearance of various forms of living beings, God

gives this kind of being the power to continue life. God is Lord
of the living, not the dead. Yet the living is nothing divine,
only creaturely. Without the sustaining power of God the
universe would "sink back into nothingness." [26] God's real
creativity is reflected only in man. The previous works assume
the form of his command. In man God began a new creation.
God's image in man means that man is free, but it is a freedom "for" something. Men are free "for" God and for one
another. The freedom of man and God's image are the same
thing. Bonhoeffer rejects the analogy of being *(analogia entis)*
for an analogy of relation *(analogia relationis)*. The analogy
of relationship is not a likeness of being, but a relation in
which freedom is given.[27] Man in freedom was to rule the
earth, but man's sin has made him the ruled. Paradoxically,
man could only rule when he was under the dominion of God.

Chapter two of Genesis is treated in the same manner.
Genesis 2 is regarded as an older account than Genesis 1, perhaps from a different source. Genesis 1 gives an account of
the transcendent God, while Genesis 2 speaks of his nearness
to man. The garden story (2:8–17) is regarded by the world
as a fantastic myth, while the church looks upon the story as
"*our* pre-history, truly our own." [28] The imagery must be
translated into "the new picture language of the technical
world," [29] but it is a story that is to be taken seriously. The
anthropomorphisms of the chapter may be offensive to modern
thinking, but the picture of Yahweh's creative activity in
forming man is important. First, it points up who made me:
God's closeness indicates concern and nearness. Second, it
shows whose I am. Regardless of how far I may run from
him, I am yet his. The ultimate concern for man is seen in
the closeness of God to man in the Incarnation.[30]

Man's origin merges two entities: spirit and matter. In
common with other creatures of the earth, man has a body of
substances. But only into man did God breathe the breath of
life. Only then was man alive. Thus man is a living body, not

a body who has a soul or a soul which has a body.

The second picture of chapter two is the garden. Two trees stand out—the tree of life and the tree of the knowledge of good and evil. The tree of life is in the middle, and Bonhoeffer speaks of our lives coming from the middle—God. Man's life circles the middle but never grasps it. Life is a gift. But man's life is real only as long as it exists in unbroken obedience. The tree of the knowledge of good and evil is set off-limits by a special word to Adam. The threat of death is joined to the command. How can Adam know the meaning of good and evil? What does this mean? To the free Adam, Bonhoeffer says, God is charting off his limitations. God is, in essence, saying, "You are a creature, Adam, be what you are." [31] Adam is limited and must live by God's grace.

Bonhoeffer states that Adam could not know, before his disobedience, the meaning of good or evil. He says that Adam was beyond good and evil.[32] But is Bonhoeffer's interpretation the correct one? Could not Adam know the meaning of good without the polarity of evil? Must we always experience evil before we know good? Did not Adam know good in knowing God? There is not a little of this in popular thinking—"you can't know the good without the evil." Why not? Evil need not be justified solely for the sake of a definition. This would require some form of eternal dualism, for God could not know evil without its existence and the experience of it. Surely Bonhoeffer is weak at this point. Bonhoeffer raises the question of how Adam could do his monstrous deed, but he cannot give an answer to this unanswerable question.

According to Bonhoeffer, the marriage statement that the husband leaves father and mother to be with his wife reflects the application of the story by the writer. But the story has meaning beyond Adam, for we are that Adam, and marriage entails the leaving of the father and mother to become one. The profundity of this union—man and woman in the community of love—is related to the church, which shows its

original form in Adam and Eve.[33] Where love exists there is
no shame. Where shame prevails it is because one person cannot accept another as the gift of God.

Genesis 3 centers on the temptation, fall, and judgment of
man. Bonhoeffer forbids the attempted identification of the
serpent with the devil. To do so is to misplace the guilt which
properly belongs only to man. This stresses also the "inconceivable, inexplicable, and inexcusable" nature of the event.
However, it is not Adam alone who is guilty, for "I have
committed evil in the midst of the primeval state of creation." [34] How this is done Bonhoeffer does not say.

The serpent's approach is to question God's word: "Did
God say . . . ?" It is assumed that evil already exists in the
world in some enigmatic form, although the creation is still
"good." The serpent asks the first religious question which
wraps evil in the garment of good. This question has contemporary significance: Did God really say that I should not
steal, commit adultery, bear false witness? Will not my case
be different from the others?

The second question undergirds the first and also contains
some truth and some falsity. God did not restrict all the fruit
of the garden, just some. But doubt was cast upon God's goodness, which helped Eve come to the point of making judg-
ments about God's Word. Man's resistance to the adversary's
question can only be met by saying "Begone, Satan" (Matt.
4:10).

The conversation progresses from statements concerning
the correctness of God's utterances to the question of why God
uttered them. The integrity of God comes under attack: God is
selfish about his existence and does not wish for you to share
it. You will not die. You will become like him. What does it
mean to become like God? It means casting off the desire to be
a creature; it means freedom, the power to create, and placing
oneself in the middle, "ordaining a new way of 'being for
God.' " [35]

Paradoxically, in wanting to be like God and gaining much

of this, man loses God, life, and harmony. The fall, or man's disobedience, results in man's rejecting limitations on himself. Sin violates the tree, the other person, and humanity in general.

Three things are to be understood about the fall, says Bonhoeffer. First, the act in the first sin is inconceivable and without excuse. Rational explanations are merely accusations that try to place the blame on the Creator. Second, once in sin, man cannot go back to unsin. Third, Adam's act is interrelated to Eve and vice versa. Thus "each man is guilty of the deed of the other." [36]

Bonhoeffer makes a startling statement about the effects of the act of disobedience: " 'The end of the ways of God is bodiliness.' " [37] The man and the woman realized, not good and evil, but their nakedness. Man's existence is ruptured to the extent that he stands ashamed before the other. No longer accepting the other person in love is shame. Bodiliness relates to sexuality also. Up to this point sexuality was not divorced from the purpose of belonging to another.[38] But now the paradox of being both an individual as well as one with another is split. "Man and woman are divided," which means that each "puts forward his claim to the possession of the other. . . . This avid passion of man for the other person first comes to expression in sexuality." [39] That is, man refuses to accept the limits of the other person. At the same time he covers himself, because nakedness is unity with the other, which is now lost.[40]

It is possible to interpret Bonhoeffer as saying that sexuality arises from the fall of man, although he does speak of it in connection with Adam and Eve in their innocence. However, he also speaks of life created through unrestrained sexuality, because man is a dying creature—man is creative in his destruction of another person. To interpret nakedness in a sexual way probably raises more questions than it answers. Was procreation possible before the fall? Bonhoeffer at one point tends to imply that sex is evil.[41]

The act of disobedience was followed by a flight into hiddenness. It is ludicrous to think that man can hide from God, but sin is never rational. Bonhoeffer calls this flight, conscience. Conscience speaks of a division in man, and conscience always puts man on the run from God. At the same time, conscience is deceptive in letting man think he can flee from God. Bonhoeffer does not equate conscience with the voice of God, but rather sees it serving as a defense against God's Word.[42] The call of God to Adam, "Where are you?" is interpreted as God's mercy attempting to keep man from hiding, from entering into self-reproach, self-torment, and religious despair. The command is for Adam to stand before God as he really is—a creature. Adam's rationalizations of his actions are reflected before God in the actions of the woman, who in turn blames the serpent.

The fall brings both a curse and a promise.[43] The opposites of pain and pleasure both become alive for Adam and Eve. This is true for their relationship with one another, in their disharmonic world, and within themselves. Man is cursed in being cut off from the tree of life. He is promised new life in Christ. This parallel of curse and promise is also seen in Eve and Mary: the first and second beginnings.

Although man is naked before God, God made for him garments. There is no exposing of man to man by God. Bonhoeffer would not have accepted the current tendencies in religious psychology to strip away all masks and forms. Some masks are necessary, and God gives the example for it in making garments for Adam and Eve. At this point, Bonhoeffer shifts from speaking of God as creator to God as preserver. Henceforth God directs the world by means of ordinances. An ordinance is a directive designed to preserve life in the sinful world.

Following the clothing of man—God's new action—man is driven out of the garden lest he eat of the tree of life and live forever. Ironically, man's desire to live forever independently of God brought his death. In his desire to be like God, man

now *is* like him—alone. God cuts off man's access to him—
sin naturally does this—and man assumes the lordship of a
world that is mute and death-producing.

The story of Adam is the story of man's history. Adam and
Eve created life—Cain, who became the first murderer. The
story repeats itself with greater intensity, for men have a
greater desire to live and hence they destroy to do it. Only in
Christ is there an end of the story in which man desires not
his own life but commits it to Christ—whose cross becomes a
tree of life—and thereby in dying to himself comes to live
forever.

Bonhoeffer's book is a profound attempt to interpret the
Genesis narrative. It must not be mistaken for a critical, exegetical attempt. It is a theological interpretation that reads
more into the accounts than is warranted. Thus the lectures
are more devotional and sermonic than theological.

Bonhoeffer raises questions which traditional theology has
answered, but which he finally skirts. The problem of the
nature of man in Eden and the interrelatedness of Adam to
mankind needs further explication. The question of the identification of the serpent, or who speaks through the serpent, and
the questions of nakedness and sexuality need further explanation. One might question whether pain itself is evil and is a
result of the fall, or whether the pain was more mental and
psychological than physical? Regardless of its weaknesses,
however, the book possesses dynamic insights into the meaning
of the first three chapters of Genesis.

PRACTICAL ADVICE ON TEMPTATION

A work quite similar to *Creation and Fall* is the shorter work
Versuchung (Temptation).[44] It repeats some of the themes
found in the former, but its occasion and setting were quite
different. The former was a series of lectures in a university
setting. *Temptation* was given over a five-day period in April

1937 to a group of clergymen of the Confessing Church to whom Bonhoeffer had been the chief mentor in the Finkenwalde seminary. The challenge to Christian living of the possibility of martyrdom—for any Christian—is posed as the ultimate threat.

The preliminary statement centers on the Lord's Prayer, "Lead us not into temptation." This plea is set over against the natural inclination of the non-Christian to assert his own strength and be victor over the enemy. The Christian realizes the real truth that in temptation one is robbed of his own staying powers. Temptation implies an abandonment—by men, by God. Man is no match for the devil. For this reason he prays, "Lead us not into temptation." Temptation is experienced on occasions. It comes like the seasons. All of life is not a temptation; the Christian also knows seasons of joy and rest in the living God.

Adam's temptation can instruct us in three things: (1) where there is innocence, there the tempter will come; (2) the tempter comes denying his origin by concealment; and (3) access to the innocent is gained by denial until the tempter has succeeded in turning the heart from God.[45] The innocence Bonhoeffer describes is "clinging to the Word of God with pure, undivided hearts." [46] The universal question that brings all men to sin is: "Has God said?"

Christ's temptation was different from Adam's—and harder. Christ assumed the burden of Adam's flesh which was under condemnation. "Even Jesus Christ . . . was born with the question: 'Has God really said?'—yet without sin." [47] Alone in the wilderness, hungry and tired, Jesus was in a sense abandoned by God, and the tempter himself—without disguise—came to assault him. The first temptation was directed to the weakness of manhood—his flesh. To satisfy the needs of hunger is legitimate, but not at the expense of losing the redemption of mankind. Jesus' reply was that he would depend upon the Word of God. The second temptation was spiritual. It was to "demand a sign from God," to charge God with guilt, to tempt God rather than lay claim to his promise and walk by faith. The third temptation Bonhoeffer designates as the "complete temptation." Jesus' allegiance to God was at stake. Satan opposed his power and rule against God's, and asked for deliberate apostasy from God.

The defense of Jesus in all three temptations was the "saving, supporting, enduring Word of God." [48] Because Jesus was tempted—and is the risen Savior—our temptation is no longer specifically our own. "Lead us not into temptation" has meaning because Christ was victor over temptation in our flesh. Because we are linked to Christ, Bonhoeffer declares that "we are not tempted, *Jesus Christ is tempted in us.*" [49] To share in his atoning life is also to share his triumph. Knowing that he has won the victory, that we are not tempted alone, gives us the help we need.

Bonhoeffer is quite to the point on the sources of temptation. The devil is the author of temptation, and his illusory claim to man is: You "can live without God's word." [50] He offers to men peace, happiness, and power—none of which he has. The devil's temptation involves separating man from God and accusing man in his sin to God. Job's temptation serves as an example of the latter. To separate man from God the devil uses robbery, sickness, and rejection. The tempted must recognize his enemy, for he can be overcome. This is done—in part—by unmasking Satan's lies.

The second source of temptation is man's lust. When the adversary is recognized, man cannot blame him for sin. Man's evil desires must be accorded the most significant role in temptation. Mine is the guilt when I say "I will."

The third source is God himself. Bonhoeffer approves of St. James's statement that God tempts no one (James 1:12, 13), but there was a real testing of men in the Old Testament. The temptation of God is his abandonment for a time of his servant. Even Satan who is in God's power is used against his

will to God's service. Satan works in three ways: (1) in temptation he leads men to see their own weaknesses; (2) he brings
suffering to the tempted; and (3) at Satan's hand the sinner
dies.[51] But when Satan works and obtains his "rights," he is
destroyed. And, more important, when man comes to a knowledge of sin and is deserving of death, he has a greater understanding of the meaning of salvation in Jesus Christ.

"Resistance to the devil is only possible in the fullest submission to the hand of God." [52] The Christian must accept
the truth of 1 Corinthians 10:13 that God will not let him be
subjected to temptations above his strength but will make a
way of escape. Thus the Christian need have no fear of temptation as long as he knows that in Christ it can be conquered.

The temptations we face parallel those of Jesus. Desire of
any kind—power, sex, fame, money—turns off joy in God for
enjoyment of creaturehood. Bonhoeffer's analysis of smolder-
ing desire, forgetfulness of God, and man's self-vindication
are incisive. Against desire one must hold to the image of the
Savior and his power. Resistance in temptation is out of the
question; fleeing is the answer. The flight to the Crucified
gives help.

The second temptation of the flesh is suffering. General
suffering is in some way connected with the devil.[53] God does
not will suffering of any kind. This is linked with sin and
man's rebellion against God—not necessarily specific sins,
but sin in general. The Christian should receive suffering in
protest against the work of the devil but at the same time use
it to strengthen faith rather than to defect from it. When Job
was deprived of everything, he rested solely in God.

Unlike general suffering, which may come to anyone, the
Christian may suffer for Christ's sake. This too is a temptation. Suffering for Christ's sake may mean one of several
things: (1) it may drive one to apostasy which would be
tragic; (2) it may drive one deeper into the arms of Christ;
(3) it may mean that one suffers the judgment of God upon

the household of faith (1 Pet. 4:18); (4) one is allowed the joy of suffering for Christ in a meaningful, purposeful way.

Man's temptations of the spirit parallel the second temptation of Jesus. Two temptations are mentioned. *Securitas* (spiritual pride) is the temptation to sin that God's grace may abound. With this is connected the hardening of the heart and a provocation of the wrath of God. *Desperatio* (despair) is the fruit of wanting to put God to the test. Inability to rest in God's promises leads to despair. Bonhoeffer's advice is practical: (1) don't argue about your sins with anyone but God; (2) remind the devil that Jesus called the sinners, not the righteous, to repentance. This last temptation is the complete one. To give in to this temptation is to make an alliance with Satan for which there is no forgiveness.

To the departing pastors, Bonhoeffer gave a final word that the defense against temptation is the armor of God described in Ephesians 6. It is God who gives, clothes, arms, and shields us. And so, Bonhoeffer says, we pray, "Lead us not into temptation" knowing that Jesus has conquered temptation for all time.

Temptation reveals the pastoral insight and concern of Bonhoeffer. This quality, expressed also in the next work, *Life Together*, serves to make Bonhoeffer attractive not only to Protestant but also to Roman Catholic readers.

V. The Church's Life in Christ

Bonhoeffer's experiences with the clandestine seminary beginning in 1935 repeat a familiar refrain in the history of the church: How can the church survive under the fire of illegality?

At Finkenwalde, Bonhoeffer ran a *Predigerseminar*, a preachers' seminary, covering a term of about six months, concentrating on pastoral duties. The days of training pastors for the Confessing Church were the most satisfying of Bonhoeffer's life. *Gemeinsames Leben (Life Together*[1]*)* is a record of this experiment. Published in 1938, the book enjoyed a popularity beyond its basic theological profundity.

Life Together deals with the practical relations of the church's life in Christ. Between the two advents of Christ the believer lives in community with other Christians. This is a gift of God; not all can experience it, for they may be scattered, imprisoned, or alone among heathen people.

THE CHRISTIAN COMMUNITY

Community, for the Christian, centers in Jesus Christ. This means three things: (1) a Christian is related to others because of Jesus Christ; (2) the path to others is only through Jesus Christ; (3) the Christian is elected in Christ from eternity to eternity.[2] The first point of being relates to one's need of others. Christians must have one another to give God's word reciprocally to each other. The word given to me is more assuring than my own. Yet my word may encourage another who is uncertain of his own heart. Thus the Christian community is to bring the message of salvation to all. The second point means that all relationships with one another and God are through Christ. He is our peace, wrote St. Paul, and the avenues to others wind through him. The third point relates to the Incarnation. We are incorporated into Christ and shall be with him and one another in an eternal fellowship.

As in his early writings, Bonhoeffer is careful to emphasize the difference between the community as an ideal and as a divine reality. The church is not the product of desire, a wish dream, or visionary hopes. If the church were a result of man's efforts, its failure would cause the founder to accuse the other members, God, and finally himself. However, the church has been created by God in Jesus Christ, and thankfulness is the only attitude open: thankfulness for forgiveness, daily provisions, and fellowship. Thankfulness is the key to greater spiritual resources. Without thankfulness for the daily gifts, the greater gifts of God will not come our way. Especially in the case of pastors, thankfulness is important. A pastor has no right to accuse his congregation before God. Rather, let him make intercession and give thanks for his congregation.

If the church is not an ideal, it is also not a human reality. As a divine reality it is also a spiritual entity which has its basis in Jesus Christ, whereas the basis of human realities is desire. In the church there is the community of those called by Christ. The fellowship of the human community is composed of devout souls and works along the lines of the magnetic persuasion of a leader. The fellowship of Christ is ruled by God's Word. In the one community the Spirit rules, in the other, psychological techniques.

Bonhoeffer's central idea is that the church as the fellowship of Christ centers on Christ rather than being a mere association of people with a common purpose. Human love and actions are related to a desire for human community. Christian love, spiritual love, comes from Christ and goes out to the other person, not directly, but through Christ. Christ "stands between me and others." [3] This means that disciplining of other people is through Christ, not directly. Direct personal influence may amount to coercion, or be an impure influence in another's life. Rather, the most direct way to another is found in prayer to Christ whose influence is greater.

The community will continue to exist only as it learns to distinguish spiritual love from human, the spiritual community from the human ideal. It "will remain sound and healthy only where it does not form itself into a movement, an order, a society, a *collegium pietatis,* but rather where it understands itself as being a part of the one, holy, catholic, Christian Church. . . ." [4] The unity of the community is in Christ. "Through him alone do we have access to one another, joy in one another, and fellowship with one another." [5]

THE COMMUNITY AT WORSHIP

Life together in the community begins with the break of day. It is proper to begin the day with worship. Worship should include thanksgiving, reading of Scripture, and prayer. To God belongs the first thought of the morning. Bonhoeffer does not lay down a rigid order of worship. But he does insist that common worship should include "the word of Scripture, the hymns of the Church, and the prayer of the fellowship." [6] His treatment shows an intense interest in the pastoral side of life.

The treatment of the Book of Psalms in worship is particularly interesting. How can one use the psalms as one's own? Can one really pray the imprecatory psalms? [7] Bonhoeffer answers that as human sinners, expressing our own evil thoughts and vengeance, we cannot. But Jesus Christ prays *all* of the psalms, and because we are in him we can follow his use of them, can pray them through him. "The Psalter is the vicarious prayer of Christ for his Church. Now that Christ is with the Father, the new humanity of Christ, the Body of Christ on earth continues to pray his prayers to the end of time. This prayer belongs, not to the individual member, but to the whole Body of Christ." [8]

Thus the Psalter can teach us how to pray because Jesus used it. The Psalter teaches us to pray according to the promises of God to his people. It teaches us also that prayer goes far beyond the experiences of the individual to the concern of Christ in the whole church. The imprecatory psalms should be used, not as individual and personal, but "as a prayer out of the heart of Jesus Christ that was sinless and clean." [9] Because our lives are in Christ, what happened to him happened to us, and herein is our right in using these prayers. The psalms direct us to a prayer fellowship. The liturgical construction of the psalms indicates this. The prayer fellowship includes fellow believers, but even where one is in prayer alone, there Christ is with him in prayer.

Although the Book of Psalms is part of the Old Testament, the reading of the Scripture needs a separate treatment. Brief readings are not a substitute for reading of the Scripture consecutively and as a whole. A family or community should read a chapter from the Old Testament and at least one half of a chapter from the New Testament daily. The Old Testament is stressed, not as dull irrelevant history, but as part of the total story of our redemption. My redemption cannot be isolated from Israel's passing through the Red Sea and other experiences. "And only in so far as we are *there*, is God with us today also." [10] Bonhoeffer goes so far as to say that what happened to Israel is more important than what God intends for me today. [11] The Scripture has prime importance for the church as well as for pastoral work. How shall one minister spiritually to others apart from the Scripture? How shall the church be guided without the Scriptures?

A part of worship is singing, and Bonhoeffer loved to sing. The beginning of the day with others involves singing. The Bible gives the precedent for singing. Singing gives the opportunity "to speak and pray the same word at the same time." Bonhoeffer advocates unison singing and speaks rather sarcastically of those who show off their musical skill by singing harmony. "Unison singing . . . is less of a musical than a spiritual matter." [12] Why? Perhaps because one concentrates on what is sung rather than on how it is sung. Here again the corporate aspect of church singing is viewed as an act of worship.

The church in prayer relates to individual and common prayer. Both formal and free prayers have their appropriate place. The fellowship of prayer means that we pray for one another's needs, give thanks for others' progress, and intercede for others' concerns.

After the day has begun with worship, the community turns to physical sustenance. Fellowship around the table means common fellowship with those of the family, or those of the community (as in the "seminary"), fellowship around the Lord's table and, finally, the ultimate fellowship in God's kingdom. In all three types there is the religious experience of knowing that life comes from God, [13] of the festive occasion in sharing food, and of sharing food with the hungry.

The community under Bonhoeffer's guidance was not without work. The first hour of the day belongs to God in worship, the other hours belong to God in work. Worship without work is as one-sided as work without worship. The day should be closed with thanksgiving and worship. Worship in the evening includes prayer for the community, the pastor, the poor, neglected, sick, dying, and for all people. The evening prayer should include also the confession of sin—both to God and to those against whom one has sinned—as well as seeking God's protection through the night when man is deep in the helplessness of sleep.

PERSONAL WORSHIP

Life Together moves from general to personal worship. Bonhoeffer warns of two extremes: "Let him who cannot be alone beware of community," and, "Let him who is not in community beware of being alone." [14] Silence is important, but it is silent obedience to the Word of God. Aloneness is necessary, but it does not become monastic. Solitude and silence have therapeutic values. After a time of quietness, one can meet people and events in a refreshed way.

Solitude and silence are important for three purposes. First, *meditation*. Meditation is the time of personal reflection on brief readings of the Scripture, not in order to sermonize, but to ask the question: what does God say to me in this text? Meditation is not a time of spiritual experimenting, a think-session for novel ideas, or a time for manufacturing unusual experiences. In meditation and through Scripture one seeks God.

Second, *prayer*. Out of meditation on Scripture comes guidance for prayer. Praying on the basis of Scripture is a means of avoiding repetition in prayer and emptiness of soul. Positively, it enables us to speak to God about matters too personal for corporate prayer. Bonhoeffer's advice concerning a wandering mind: pray for the subjects of the straying thoughts and use this as a means of enlarging one's prayer concerns.

Third, *intercession*. To bring one's brother into the presence of God in concern for his needs is to intercede for him. The Christian fellowship lives or dies by what it does in intercession. Intercession is the means of transforming one's personal attitudes about other people. It is hard to hate one you talk with God about. The intercession of the Christian is a service owed to God and man. Such intercession is more meaningful and fruitful the more definite it is. The importance of this service demands that it be diligently protected by a special time that is regular.

The real test of meditation comes in the crucible of daily experience. Has it made one strong or weak? What happens to the individual affects the community. If the individual is weak, then a sickness invades the community. Bonhoeffer's beatitude is poignant: "Blessed is he who is alone in the strength of the fellowship and blessed is he who keeps the fellowship in the strength of aloneness." [15]

TYPES OF MINISTRIES

Bonhoeffer turns next to the ministry and its problems. He analyzes the disciples' bickering about who should be the greatest among them (Luke 9:46) from the standpoint of advantage, of personal gain, and of power. The struggle for advantage is a rejection of justification by faith in favor of self-justification.[16]

The Christian must learn to *hold his tongue*. Evil thoughts are defeated most effectively when they are never reduced to words. In the control of the tongue, personal advice to another is not prohibited, but at the same time criticism must not be offered under the cloak of advice. Criticism is generally a technique used to gain advantage over the other person. We should rather recognize the other person as free in the image of God.

The freedom of each person is necessary for the community. If the fellowship is divided by criticism into the advantaged and the disadvantaged, it will be the death of the community. The strong cannot survive without the weak, but the weak must not be regarded as inferior without their own proper work. "A community which allows unemployed members to exist within it will perish because of them." [17] Each person must have purpose, use, and a contribution to make to the life of the community. There can be no superfluous people.

The ministry of *meekness* follows the ministry of holding one's tongue. Learning to think of others as deserving and having more honor is meekness. Receiving forgiveness of sin teaches us that we have reached the end of our own way of self-seeking and have cast aside self-righteousness. Seeking honor is detrimental to faith, for honor-seeking is self-centered where faith is Christ-centered. Resentment in the community is the product of honor-seeking.

The meek person not only puts aside self-conceit but also associates with the lowly and in doing so declares himself to be the greatest of sinners. The meek will not excuse his own sins, but will be forgiving in regard to others. Bonhoeffer asks, "How can I possibly serve another person in unfeigned humility if I seriously regard his sinfulness as worse than my own?" [18]

In reaching out to others there is the ministry of *listening*. Learning to listen is a vital ministry for Christians and especially clergymen. More inclined to contribute to the point of prattling, the Christian must recapture the art of listening. Listening must be genuine, not the kind that is waiting with half an ear ready to pour out a barrage of answers to other's problems. Impatient listening is a form of despising other people. Bonhoeffer decries the surrender of therapeutic listening to secular education, because it is an art committed to the Christian by God. But Christians have not been listening to others, and when we do not listen to them we do not hear God.

The ministry of *helpfulness* is another community activity. "This means, initially, simple assistance in trifling, external matters." [19] When one is too busy to help in the lowliest of services, one is guilty of taking a career too seriously. God sends people our way to interrupt us. Their claims are urgent and we must be obedient in ministering to them. We must not be the priest who passes by on the other side reading the

Bible. Bonhoeffer compares the monk's vow of obedience to his abbot to one's service obligation to one's brother. In either case our time is not our own. We are God's to serve others.

The ministry of *bearing* means "forbearing and sustaining."[20] If the Christian does not bear the burden of his brother, how is he different from the pagan? Christ bore our burdens, and we in turn are to bear one another's burdens. The entire Christian life is that of cross-bearing. If we refuse to bear the burdens of others, we are not bearing the cross. Bearing the other's burdens may mean accepting him in his freedom and involving a clash with another's personality, yet God has not given permission to remake any man in *our* image.

Bearing the burdens of others means we are not to judge others, and are to guard against malicious glee over another's failure, whether that one is strong or weak. Conversely, it means that whoever needs to be lifted up will receive help. The ministry of bearing may involve forgiving the sins of one's brother. But when the community is shattered by the sin of one, who is not at fault? It is not his sin alone, but the sin of all who have not interceded in prayer, have failed to give counsel when needed, or have neglected their ministry in the community.

It is only when we have learned to minister on the above levels that we are ready for the ministry of *proclaiming*. Proclaiming in this context is not related to the pulpit or the ordained ministry, but refers to the communication of the gospel from person to person. This is the free encounter born out of a relationship where one has truly listened, served, and borne the needs of others. Without this prior ministry, Bonhoeffer declares that our message has already been contradicted.

He raises genuine questions about probing into the sacred life of another. The other person "has his own right, his own responsibility, and even his own duty, to defend himself against unauthorized interference."[21] Yet God may hold us responsible for our brother's life blood.

Against our personal hesitancy, our Christian duty is to help. The word we utter is based upon the premise of not denying our brother his needs. Can we deny help and aid to one who is, as we are, a sinner and stands in danger of judgment? Do we not grant him dignity by declaring that he can be reconciled to God? Would we be Christian to be silent while he faces destruction?

If we are to be obedient to God's word, we cannot stand idle while our brother falls into sin. Bonhoeffer says that reproof is necessary, for "the practice of discipline in the congregation begins in the smallest circles. Where defection from God's Word in doctrine or life imperils the family fellowship and with it the whole congregation, the word of admonition and rebuke must be ventured. Nothing can be more cruel than the tenderness that consigns another to his sin." [22]

Rebuke is simply to call back to the common fellowship. The ministry of rebuking is always in relation to God. Only God can reclaim a person, but he chooses to work through us. His Word must be spoken by us, and through it God works to bring the erring brother to repentance.

When the above qualities of ministering are incarnate in a person, he will minister with authority. Bonhoeffer is critical of the personality cult so frequent in the ministry, whereby people are attached to the man rather than the office. There is authority in the office, but not in the personal glamor of the man. The description in 1 Timothy of the bishop has nothing to say about brilliance, but much about simplicity, faithfulness, sound doctrine, and Christian living. Pastoral authority arises when the ministry admits that it has no authority save that of Christ and his Word.

A PROPOSAL FOR A PROTESTANT CONFESSIONAL

In the last theme, intriguing support is given to confession. From the standpoint of Protestantism, this is a most interesting chapter. Bonhoeffer states:

The pious fellowship permits no one to be a sinner. So every-
body must conceal his sin from himself and from the fellowship. We dare not be sinners. Many Christians are unthink-
ably horrified when a real sinner is suddenly discovered
among the righteous.[23]

So what do we do? We cover up our sin, and live in hypocrisy.
In contrast to this kind of fellowship, the gospel is only for
the sinner. We do not have to lie but we can own up to God.
Moreover, we are to confess and be confessed to.

The importance of confession centers around the nature of
sin. "Sin demands to have a man by himself." [24] It isolates
him, by desiring to remain unknown. Where there is confession, the way is open for returning to the community. In confession one gives up his evil, gives his heart to God, and
finds forgiveness and fellowship. Confession should be on a
personal basis between two people, not necessarily to the
entire church, for in confession to one member confession is
made to all. If there is confession, the sinner is never alone
again.

Confession is important for it declares something about
ourselves. It says that we are not afraid to be linked with
Christ and the ignominy of his death. If we refuse this link we
will probably refuse to confess our sins, in which case there is
no help. In confession, one experiences depths of humiliation,
but it is in humiliation that God conquers man. In confession
there is born the joy of forgiveness in Christ.

Confession to a brother is a way of certainty. It guards
against self-confession. Confessing my sin to God alone may
be merely mental gymnastics whereby I grant myself forgiveness without true confession. It may also explain my feeble-
ness in overcoming sin and the resultant relapses that occur.
God's forgiveness is spoken to me through my brother as I
confess to him.

Meaningful confession must concentrate on specific sins.
Therefore self-examination as preparation for confession will

use the Ten Commandments. In confession one is dealing with real problems, and thus real forgiveness is sought.

To whom shall one confess? Bonhoeffer's answer is: "He who himself lives beneath the Cross." [25] Why not a psychologist? The latter knows human weakness, but not godlessness. He knows something of man's nature, but not his sin. Only the Christian knows this and knows the need of forgiveness and can pronounce it for God.

There are two dangers in confession. One who hears confessions may regard them as routine. Only those who confess should hear confessions, thus keeping confession from becoming mere form or routine. Bonhoeffer warns the confessant against regarding confession as a pious work, for "confession as a pious work is an invention of the devil." [26] But confession rightly used and understood involves God's offer of grace.

Confession is, finally, related to the holy Communion. Jesus commanded that all should come to worship after they have reconciled themselves with their brother. Before the Lord's Supper is received there should be general confession on the part of the fellowship. When confession is ended, forgiveness is declared and the people of God share in the fellowship of the table that will be perfected in eternity.

In assessment we must say that Bonhoeffer shows remarkable pastoral insight. *Life Together* may be regarded as a prolegomena to a minister's manual. Much more would have to be developed, but it serves well as the foundation. However, certain questions need to be raised about Bonhoeffer's views in this book. First, he has Luther's propensity to see Christ everywhere in the Old Testament, particularly in the Psalms. This leads to considerable allegorization of the Scripture under the guise of "theological interpretation." Most interpreters of Scripture regard this as suspect, because it goes beyond the historical-grammatical-critical standard of Scripture interpretation. In this Bonhoeffer follows Luther.

Second, his comments on unison singing seem to be purely

aesthetic, and, for American readers, arbitrary. We should remember, however, that German Lutheran churches do not use music for the hymnbooks in the pews, so that it is possible for someone singing parts to be actually showing off his ability, as well as being in danger of singing the wrong notes. For many people, on the other hand, singing in parts is more natural and fitting to one's voice range. It is also possible to show off in unison singing.

Third, while Bonhoeffer has many valuable thoughts on confession, he is too one-sided in his approach. He admits that one may have "certainty, new life, the Cross, and fellowship without benefit of confession to a brother," [27] but he is concerned with those who need it. The manner of treatment may suggest that most people need confession to another. His treatment is an improvement on the usual Roman Catholic view in which confession is normally relegated to the priestly office. But is there not a danger that psychological benefits may be mistaken for spiritual relief? Does not confession displace the promise and Word of God with a word of a man?

VI. The Church's
Brand of Discipleship

Bonhoeffer's most famous work published during his lifetime
was *The Cost of Discipleship (Nachfolge)*, which achieved a
wide reputation for him. It is a serious work and in some ways
a work of "hard sayings." It contains a profound interpretation of the Sermon on the Mount plus an exposition of Matthew 9:35–10:42, and sections on the "Church of Jesus
Christ" and the "Life of Discipleship."

WHAT IS DISCIPLESHIP?

The important question is: What does it mean to follow Jesus
Christ? Bonhoeffer fears that many do not follow for the
wrong reasons; for instance, a human rather than the divine
word is preached; offense is taken at the "superstructure of
human, institutional, and doctrinal elements in our preaching" [1] rather than at the Word of God. He calls for a return
to Scripture and to Jesus Christ, and he therefore proposes
"to tell how Jesus calls us to be his disciples." [2] Discipleship
is much easier than man-made rules and dogmas, but more
important, what Jesus asks, he gives the grace to do. Discipleship may be hard, but it is not limited to a small spiritual
elite. Discipleship is the road to Christian joy.

The background for the exposition of the Sermon on the
Mount is the prevalence in the church of what Bonhoeffer calls

75

"cheap grace." Cheap grace has brought chaos to the church. It is defined in several ways: intellectual assent to a doctrine or idea; justification of the sinner without a corresponding change in his ethic; but perhaps the greatest passage is the following:

> Cheap grace is the preaching of forgiveness without requiring repentance, baptism without church discipline, Communion without confession, absolution without personal confession. Cheap grace is grace without discipleship, grace without the cross, grace without Jesus Christ, living and incarnate.[3]

Grace, on the other hand, is dear and costly. A man must give up his life to follow Christ. Grace is dear because it cost the Son of God his life, but it is grace because God did not count this too great a cost.

Cheap grace arose as the church became secularized and the world became Christianized. Costly grace did not die, as is evidenced in the rise of the monastic movement wherein the spiritual elite yet retained something of the demands of discipleship. But even the cloister was a corruption of grace. The life of a disciple is to be lived in the world against its hostility, not in the favored atmosphere of a friendly monastery. Against the triumph of cheap grace in the church, Bonhoeffer calls for a return to obedience of Christ. Only in costly grace is there joy in Christian living.

How does one become a disciple? First, there is the call of Jesus to follow *him*. A doctrinal system, a church structure, and other substitutes for the Living Christ render discipleship irrelevant.[4] Second, in answering the call of Christ one must take the first concrete step. This step takes one out of his previous existence and places him where faith is possible. "Faith can no longer mean sitting still and waiting—they must arise and follow him." [5]

At this juncture Bonhoeffer introduces two propositions that must be held together always. Both are equally true: *"Only he who believes is obedient, and only he who is obedient believes."* [6] There is no obedience without faith nor faith without obedience. In believing there is an act of obedience, such as Peter's leaving his nets or Matthew's walking away from his receipts. This act of obedience is never more than a "dead work of the law" [7] but it must be done because Jesus commands it. Inability to believe is probably due to unwillingness to take the first step.

Bonhoeffer's pastoral concern shows in the hypothetical instance of a man who says he wants to believe and cannot. The usual pastor is baffled about the next step in his presentation. The secret weapon is to continue the dialogue by saying, " 'Only those who obey, believe. . . . You are disobedient, you are trying to keep some part of your life under your own control.' " [8] If you give up your sins, your uncommitted world, and obey, you will believe.

Many of the questions raised about believing are "dodges" for obeying. Theoretical questions of reservations about the law and its application and interpretation are described by Bonhoeffer as devices to avoid obedience to Christ. The account of the rich young man (Matt. 19:16–22) or the lawyer of the Good Samaritan story are used as examples of people who asked questions in order to avoid the demands of discipleship.

Bonhoeffer's insight into the rewards of discipleship are deep. In discipleship one is seemingly dragged into insecurity which in reality turns into the safety of Christ. Following Christ means leaving the world of the finite and being brought into the life of the Infinite.[9] We are called to attach ourselves exclusively to his person. Jesus' call is without qualification. There is only one way of understanding Jesus: he meant it as he said it. All subterfuges based on "reason and conscience, responsibility and piety" stand in the way of complete obedience.[10] The usual type of rationalization of the commands of

Christ are dealt with mercilessly. This refers to the reasoning whereby we reinterpret Jesus to mean that we need not leave all, but simply possess the wealth of the world as though we did not possess it. The command to follow is reduced to developing a spirit of inward detachment. Instead, nothing must stand in our way of fulfilling the command of Christ. Nor must we abandon the "single-minded understanding of the commandment." [11] When single-mindedness is neglected, cheap grace sneaks back into the religious life. Likewise, when the principle of simple obedience is thrown out, an unevangelical interpretation of the Bible takes the place of the truly evangelical. Bonhoeffer defends the literal interpretation of the Bible,[12] not in order to establish legalism or letterism, "but to proclaim Christ." At the same we cannot behave as though we were contemporary with the disciples. Merely giving up possessions is not to be confused with obedience to Jesus. Becoming a Franciscan bound to poverty may be the farthest from following Jesus.

Being a disciple is related to bearing the cross of Christ. Suffering and rejection go hand in hand with bearing the cross. Suffering alone could produce a martyr, but rejection prohibits it. To take up the cross is to deny oneself. "To deny oneself is to be aware only of Christ and no more of self, to see only him who goes before and no more the road which is too hard for us." [13] Every Christian must bear the cross. The cross means (1) that one must "abandon the attachments of this world," (2) that one must come after Christ and die to himself, and (3) perhaps undergo death completely. Suffering is one of the badges of discipleship. Yet in suffering there is triumph. When suffering is concluded there is nothing else it can do. It is a path to victory.

There is a paradox discovered in answering the call of Christ. In discipleship "men become individuals." [14] Before this they stood under the façade of responsibilities, duties, and relationships to the world. But the call of Christ demands a break with the world as well as with the past. Christ's call places a barrier between man and the world. Man must forsake the world, but in doing so he learns that he never really knew the world. In Christ he finds a new relation possible between himself and God, between himself and man, between himself and reality. All relationships now are to be mediated through Christ. Being in Christ, it becomes possible to see how isolated man is from man. It is impossible to know another person directly. Because Christ now stands between man and neighbor, the shortest and most direct way to the neighbor is through Christ. "That is why intercession is the most promising way to reach our neighbours, and corporate prayer, offered in the name of Christ, the purest form of fellowship." [15]

As an example of this, Bonhoeffer uses the story of Abraham. To answer God's call, Abraham turned his back upon his father's house and became a pilgrim in hopes of a promised land. In the command to sacrifice his son, a barrier is placed between Abraham and Isaac. Isaac is given back but something is different. Abraham now has Isaac "through the Mediator and for the Mediator's sake." [16] The outward details are still the same, but a new relationship has arisen and the reality is different. Abraham also serves as an example of a man becoming an individual in the midst of his own people and with the enjoyment of wealth. This type of individuality is harder, for it is easier to return to the way of direct relationships with people and forfeit our discipleship in Christ.

However, only Christ can determine which path we will take, says Bonhoeffer. Christ not only makes new individuals but he calls to a new fellowship wherein he stands between the members. The fellowship of the church takes precedence over the house, father, mother, or brothers that are left behind. The reward is hundredfold over what is forsaken. But included in the reward is the promise "with persecutions."

The seriousness of the call of Christ is realistically set forth in all its hardness: deny yourself, accept persecutions, forsake all. But he who calls gives strength to endure. Surely Bonhoeffer's life is a poignant example of this statement.

THE SERMON ON THE MOUNT

Bonhoeffer takes the beatitudes seriously. There is one place where the beatitudes are incarnate in one person—the crucified of Golgotha. Thus the disciples, following their Lord, "are called blessed because they have obeyed the call of Jesus." [17] The *poor in spirit* are those who have accepted the loss of all things including their own selves for his sake. Those who *mourn* are those who do "without what the world calls peace and prosperity." [18] Mourning means to refuse to be in harmony with the standards of the world. The *meek* are those who give up claims to their own rights for the will of Christ. Those who *hunger and thirst for righteousness* are those renouncing all claims to personal achievement, who wait for God's reign of righteousness. The *merciful*, having given up claims to their own dignity, become "men for others," helping the needy, sick, castouts—all those who need any kind of ministry. The *pure in heart* become that way by giving their hearts completely to the reign of Jesus. Under his rule, he purifies their hearts with his Word. The *peacemakers* renounce all violence and "maintain fellowship where others would break it off." [19] The persecuted for righteousness suffer for "any just cause" [20] and will be rejected by the world, but God's kingdom belongs to them. To this motley crew the world says "Away with them" and God agrees with the world. But he intends them for the kingdom of heaven, where their reward is great.

The disciples, the blessed ones, are not too good for the world, for they are thrust into its center as the salt of the earth. The kingdom of heaven is theirs only after they finish their earthly task. For the disciple there are only two options: being the salt of the earth or being annihilated and crushed.

Similarly, as the lights of the world they receive energy from the light of the cross. The bushels that cover men's light—whether fear, ulterior motives, or humane causes—go to the heart of determining whether one is Christian or not. If the light does not shine can there be oneness with Christ?

The close connection with Christ distinguishes the disciples from the Pharisees. Both stand under the obligation to keep the Old Testament law. The Pharisee tried and failed. Hence Jesus spoke of the need of a "better righteousness." The disciple begins his keeping of the law in reference to Jesus Christ who fulfilled it completely, both by living in complete communion with God and by dying a sinner's death on the cross. He becomes thereby the righteousness of the disciples. Their fulfilling of the law which exceeds the Pharisees's keeping of the law is not in terms of personal achievement. They can only exceed the righteousness of the Pharisees by receiving the gift of righteousness, the fulfiller of the law, Christ himself.

Bonhoeffer declares it to be false to separate the law from the disciple. He is not free of it anymore than he is free of God because he is in Christ. He says, "There is no fulfilment of the law apart from communion with God, and no communion with God apart from fulfilment of the law." [21] The Jews committed the first error and the disciples were tempted to the second. Discipleship is not to be confused with obeying the law, but disobeying the law removes one from being a disciple. [22] As the Divine Lawgiver, Jesus corrected some of the erroneous usages of the law. A chief correction comes in the matter of legalism. The real meaning of the law is explained.

The commandment on killing relates not only to the overt act but to attitudes of anger and hate as well as insult. Bonhoeffer rejects the subtle distinction between "righteous indignation and unjustifiable anger." [23] Rather freedom from anger is the command for the disciple. Anger hinders worship and prohibits service. The church fellowship must not copy the

world in its ways of contempt and contumely. We cannot
honor God and dishonor our brother. To honor God requires
a reconciliation against all that have been offended. Being
permitted to make this reconciliation is part of God's grace.
Over against our making up stands the court of judgment.

The commandment on adultery is related to desire where
there is no love. Discipleship forbids a free rein of lust. If the
disciple retains his gaze upon Christ his gaze will be pure even
when looking at a woman. Bonhoeffer interprets Jesus as sanctifying marriage along with its indissolubility. The intent of
both Jesus and the law was to safeguard marriage. Any violation of the law—in any sexual irregularity—is against the
Body of Christ because the disciple is a member of his Body.
To be dead to lust and desire is possible because in Christ the
disciple was crucified, or put to death, and desire has no hold
on a dead person.

The command prohibiting the use of oaths is accepted by
Bonhoeffer without the Reformation exception of the state in
a court of law. Discipleship means complete truthfulness. Discipleship supposes that one has been completely truthful with
Jesus, else there is no forgiveness. Truthfulness is the basis
of fellowship among believers. Without it the brotherhood is
destroyed.

Bonhoeffer is most interesting when he treats the revenge
passage of Matthew 5:38–42. He is dead serious about this
part of the Sermon. His passive resistance views are evident.
The Old Testament nation of Israel was a political as well as
religious community, and retribution was necessary. But the
new community is religious only. The way to conquer evil,
then, is not politically but passively. If the disciple is meek,
not counting his own rights, he will not seek redress when
wronged. Resistance creates further resistance and solves
nothing. Bonhoeffer knows of no exception at this point in his
writing. "There is no deed on earth so outrageous as to justify
a different attitude. The worse the evil, the readier must the

Christian be to suffer. . . ." [24] Bonhoeffer rejects the Reformation distinction between suffering as a Christian and suffering due to holding an office or performing a duty. He asks, "Am I ever acting only as a private person or only in an official capacity?" [25] This must not be interpreted to make nonresistance a rule for secular life. For so interpreted, God's ordinances for preserving the world would be rejected. Rather the civil order has its directions for life while the disciple has a different order. The strong pacifism here is remarkably in contrast to Bonhoeffer's later involvement in the resistance to the Nazi regime as well as his involvement in the plot to assassinate Hitler. His later view did not come easily.

Following the rejection of the *lex talionis* [26] Bonhoeffer turns to the "extraordinary" feature in the disciple—the love of the enemy. This is the only way to overcome him. The Christian cannot return hostility for hostility; Jesus does not allow this. The greater the hatred, the greater the love must be for the hater. Loving the enemy is to serve him "in all things without hypocrisy and with utter sincerity. No sacrifice which a lover would make for his beloved is too great for us to make for our enemy." [27] The extraordinary feature is that it goes beyond mere love of friend for friend. This is taken for granted. Jesus commands that love for the enemy be a hallmark of the disciple. This love is the fulfilling of the law and obedience to Christ.

Chapter five of Matthew relates to the openness of the disciple's life. Chapter six speaks of the hiddenness of his spiritual existence. What is meant? The hiddenness is from *ourselves*. [28] Discipleship means looking at and following Christ. When one begins to notice his own love and goodness, one ceases being a disciple. The disciple's life includes prayer. Not a natural activity, prayer must be taught, and Jesus does not leave his disciples in ignorance. They pray because they are commanded, but always through a Mediator. Access to

God is only through a mediator. Prayer is never an entreaty—
for God knows our needs—nor is it a pious work. It has a
hidden character, for in prayer men "have ceased to know
themselves, and know only God whom they call upon." [29]
The place or time of prayer is not important, for even in a
private room one may make a nice display of himself in
prayer. The model prayer Jesus gave his disciples is the
"quintessence of prayer." [30] It serves to place boundaries
around the disciple's prayer.

A practice akin to prayer is fasting. Bonhoeffer follows
Jesus' warning against mere pious fasting to impress either
others or oneself. Fasting has the motive of self-discipline for
better service to Christ. The objections to fasting—the resistance of the flesh and "evangelical liberty"—must not deter
one from fasting as a form of discipline. [31] When the Christian
has failed in obedience, is guilty of sin against others, has
lost the joy of Christian grace, and has come to little or no
prayer, he needs to fast and pray. There is the danger, however, of trying to "imitate the sufferings of Christ." This
reduces itself to "a desire for ostentation" and hence must be
rejected. [32]

Moving from fasting to "the simplicity of the carefree
life," Bonhoeffer stresses the singleness of following Christ
alone. It is never Christ *and* something else. Singleness of
heart relates both to treasures on earth and to what master we
serve. Treasures are a part of human nature. Rather than be
denied them, the disciple is given "higher objects—the glory
of God (John 5:44), the glorying in the cross (Gal. 6:14),
and the treasure in heaven." [33] Singleness of heart relates to
the master we serve: God or Mammon. We must love God or
hate him.

The first two chapters of the Sermon (Matt. 5 and 6) display the uniqueness of the disciple. Because of his extraordi-

nary position, how is he to be related to the non-Christian? This subject receives treatment in Matthew 7, or the third section of the Sermon. No superior attitude is warranted, for the believer possesses his righteousness as gift, not by achievement. If he judges, God will judge him, for in his judgment he gives up the meaning of discipleship. There is no vantage point for the disciple. Rather he must come to the non-Christian with "an unconditional offer of fellowship, with the single-mindedness of the love of Jesus." [34] If we are inclined to judge so that evil might be destroyed, we should look within ourselves.

As judgment is prohibited, so is coercion in making disciples of other people. Proselytizing is wrong for three reasons: (1) swine do not recognize costly pearls; (2) "it profanes the word of forgiveness"; (3) it does not recognize the weakness of the gospel. [35] The disciple has no power over the other person except through Christ in prayer. This alone is a powerful hope. The church will not win the majority of mankind. Many are on the road to destruction. For the disciple the road is narrow and many are the ways of losing oneself. "But if we behold Jesus Christ going on before step by step, we shall not go astray." [36] The disciple's separation from the world is not permanent. Discipleship must be renewed daily. Following is made all the harder because there are false prophets who look, act, and speak like Christians. Here one cannot judge but must wait for evil to show its colors.

The division of the true from the false will be done by God himself. The great final judgment involves all, and division will hinge on those who confess him and those who do not. Presently, there is possibility of a demonic confession devoid of love, without Christ, and without the Spirit of God. The important question is: "Who will pass the test and who will not?" [37] Bonhoeffer's answer is that "the word of the last judgment is foreshadowed in the call to discipleship. . . . If we follow Christ, cling to his word, and let everything else go, it will see us through the day of judgment. His word is his grace." [38]

Following Bonhoeffer's exposition of the Sermon on the Mount, he gives an exposition of Matthew 9:35–10:42. [39] Short vignettes are drawn of the *harvest* (the people are without a shepherd, without relief, deliverance, and forgiveness) for which one must pray for laborers; the *call* of the apostles (who are given power stronger than Satan's and are bound together only by their choice and call); the *work* (fulfilling their commission to preach, traveling as messengers of the King, living in "royal poverty," warning men of the urgency of the times); the *suffering* of the messengers (as Jesus was persecuted so the messengers will be, but they are forewarned; because Christ will return the disciples are not to fear man, or to be gullible in thinking that "there is good in every man" [40]); the *decision* (man's eternal destiny is determined by his decision on earth for the devil or for Christ); and the *fruit* (the disciples are fellow workers having as their goal the "salvation of the Church"). [41]

DISCIPLESHIP TODAY

Part Four of *The Cost of Discipleship* is entitled, "The Church of Jesus Christ and the Life of Discipleship." Is there a difference between being a disciple when Jesus was alive and being one today? Are we moderns not in a more difficult situation when we do not have the personalized call to follow Jesus? How are we to decide what following Jesus may mean for us, or to know for sure that we are not following our own wishes?

Bonhoeffer rejects these questions and similar ones as being wrong. Jesus yet lives. The resurrection is a fact, and Jesus calls to the modern to follow him. Where is he to be found? "The preaching of the Church and the administration of the

sacraments is the place where Jesus Christ is present."[42]
Jesus never calls to a one specific action, but to decisive discipleship—a decision for or against following him. How are
we to discern which commands of his are related to us? This
question is based upon a misunderstanding. "The object of
Jesus' command is always the same—to evoke whole-hearted
faith, to make us love God and our neighbour with all
our heart and soul. This is the unequivocal feature in his
command."[43]

Moving from the Gospels to the epistles, Bonhoeffer maintains that the terminology is different but expresses the same
concept. "Baptism" is the Pauline equivalent of "following
Christ." "Baptism" is essentially passive—*being baptized,
suffering* the call of Christ."[44] Baptism involves the same
breach with the world as following Christ. In baptism, one
dies to the old world. In baptism, "Christ invades the realm
of Satan, lays hands on his own and creates for himself his
Church."[45] The demand of Christ for a visible act of obedience is manifested in the public act of baptism. Although
Bonhoeffer seems to admit the possibility of apostasy and
hence a return to Christ, he professes a finality about baptism.
It may not be repeated.[46]

These views seem to point up a sharp difficulty in Bonhoeffer. On the one hand, Christ calls for a decision which
can only be related to responsiveness. On the other Bonhoeffer
defends infant baptism[47] which lacks a response and intimates
a coercion which he had previously rejected. However Bonhoeffer insists that there must be a "firm faith present" (which
"can only happen in a living Christian community") before
the sacrament be administered. In this matter he makes no
progress beyond Luther, who never successfully resolved this
antinomy.

The first disciples lived in the presence of Jesus. Is there a
Pauline counterpart? Decidedly so! To be a member of the
Body of Christ by baptism is to have a better relation than the

disciples, for it is the glorified Lord with whom we have to
do. Bonhoeffer's reasoning follows traditional forms here.
Adam and Christ are individuals and representatives of man.
In one the race fell into sin, in the second there is created a
new humanity.[48] All men are in one or the other or both. The
Incarnate Word took to himself sinful flesh (which Bonhoeffer
defines only as "human nature" or "our infirmities and . . .
our sin"[49]) and thereby sought to create a community of fol-
lowers. How is one incorporated into this community, this
body? "The answer is through the two sacraments of his Body,
baptism and the Lord's Supper."[50] Preaching alone will not
do it; the sacraments are necessary.

The Body of Christ, the church, takes Christ's place until
he comes. Thus the church is not an institution, but a person.[51]
Bonhoeffer notes that there is unity between Christ and the
church as his Body, but there can be no mystic fusion of the
two because Christ is still the Head of the Body—a metaphor
which speaks of his Lordship over the church. We do share in
his sufferings—we may suffer for him and for his church.
The church is the fulfillment of ancient prophecy. The tem-
ples at Jerusalem were not built by God nor did they endure.
God's true temple will endure forever and it finds its fullest
meaning in the body of Christ which is the living temple of
God.[52]

In a chapter on "The Visible Community" Bonhoeffer
returns to a familiar theme developed in the *Communion of
Saints*. The "Body of Christ" is visible on earth and has
spatial relationships. An idea, a thought, a truth does not
require space, but a body does. The church is made visible in
the preaching of the Word of God and in the sacraments. The
Word is shared with the community and the world, while the
sacraments are restricted to the believers. There are other
offices and services in the church, but the "uncorrupted ministry of the Word and Sacraments is of paramount importance."[53] Because the church is visible it must have living

space. Its daily life must be permitted to exist. When the church is continually circumscribed in its existence, then the end will be near.[54]

The church has obligations to society. Christians are not revolutionaries because "revolution would only obscure that divine New Order which Jesus has established. It would also hinder and delay the disruption of the existing world order in the coming of the kingdom of God." [55] Rather they must be in subjection to the higher powers as Paul asserts (Rom. 13:1ff.). Bonhoeffer seems to prohibit high office to the Christian, because the Christian is a servant. The Christian must do good no matter what the world about him is doing. Should he suffer for it, he was warned of such by Christ. In his vocation, the Christian works within the framework of what is compatible to the Body of Christ. His livelihood, his way of life, his marriage is accepted only within the framework of being a pilgrim, not a resident of the world.

The people who make up the visible community are the *saints*. How does a holy God have a relation to a sinful people? The answer lies in his act of atonement and justification of the sinner. In the Incarnation God assumes sinful flesh and dies the death of all flesh.[56] In turn the obedience and righteousness of Christ become that of the formerly alienated. This is the significance of the historical Incarnation. The present believer achieves this incorporation into Christ through baptism.[57]

Once within the fellowship of Christ, the saints must renew daily the meaning of their baptism. Sanctification is the concern of the justified. To be sanctified is to fulfill the command to be holy. Bonhoeffer treats sanctification in three aspects of the saints' lives: (1) holy living will be achieved only by not being conformed to the world; (2) Christian living will be a result of walking with Christ; (3) "their sanctification will be *hidden*, and they must *wait* for the day of Jesus Christ." [58]

In his discussion of sanctification Bonhoeffer speaks of sin, church discipline, and good works. Sin may be of two kinds: moral and intellectual. Moral sin is headed by whoredom which is a form of idolatry.[59] Intellectual, doctrinal sin is more serious for it corrupts the gospel. Moral sin leaves the gospel of forgiveness intact.[60] Church discipline takes several forms: personal exhortation, pulpit warnings, and church action of exclusion. This is consistent with his overall theme of ridding the church of cheap grace. Good works are necessary, for God demands them. Yet "our good works are the works of God himself."[61] It is the doers of the law who shall be justified in judgment. Thus Bonhoeffer does not draw a sharp distinction between faith and works. "It is evil works rather than good works which hinder and destroy faith."[62]

Bonhoeffer concludes *The Cost of Discipleship* with a return to God's beginning point. God created man in his own image. Because of man's sin this is effaced. Christ came to renew God's work of his image in man. Man could not achieve renewal himself. Thus God effects it. The image will reach its final form in the resurrection where the transforming will be complete.

The Cost of Discipleship still stands as a much needed book. Its greatness must not be detracted from by criticisms which show its one-sidedness or weakness. A man must be appreciated for what he says positively, rather than censored for weaknesses. It is easy to focus on the disagreements one has with a writer. We hope we may be forgiven for doing that here.

In his books relating to the church, Bonhoeffer dissociates himself from "the fanatics and enthusiasts," a term equated with pietists and probably those of the Anabaptist tradition. "Fanatics and enthusiasts" often referred to those peoples and movements who made up the "radical reformation," that part of the reformation more extreme than the Lutheran and Calvinist movements. These people, along with the pietists of later times, stressed personal faith and experience over against a sacramental and liturgical view of the church. Bonhoeffer charges these people with perfectionism.[63] This charge appears contradictory to his own position in some ways. In some instances he held positions similar to those of the fanatics (pietists or Anabaptists)—for instance, his attitude toward the holding of high office in government.[64]

It might be ventured that the Anabaptist or pietist had a better answer to certain aspects of the Christian life than Bonhoeffer. The issue of baptism may serve as an example. The cheap grace mentality that Bonhoeffer censored came in part from the long-held practice of baptizing infants. Infant baptism became a cultural rather than a religious event which glossed over personal faith and commitment. Religion that begins in the unconsciousness of infancy often remains unconscious. This is the cultural milieu out of which Bonhoeffer's criticism arises.

While Bonhoeffer saw the lack of commitment, many of these "fanatics" saw infant baptism as breeding cheap grace. They stressed the importance of faith, of adult commitment; thus grace was "costly" to them. Following Christ meant forsaking the world. Their danger lay in the direction of legalism. Bonhoeffer denounced legalism, but "costly grace" may lead one in that direction.

There is a dilemma in the Christian life remaining to be negotiated as long as we have perception. On the one hand, there is slavish legalism, in which the commands of Scripture are adhered to with deep concern for fulfillment and obedience, even though obedience may be perfunctory. On the other hand, there is the freedom of Christ which delivers from punctiliousness but which may slide in the direction of disobedience to Christ's commands. The Christian has to probe for the channel that will take him through life in the joyful freedom of Christ where the commands of God are found to be meaningful for his own welfare. I am not sure that Bonhoeffer escapes the problems he saw in the pietist tradition. It may be that he was nearer the pietists in terms of costly grace than he realized.

Again, his treatment of good works leaves something to be desired. He did not achieve a synthesis of good works and faith anymore than he did on baptism and faith. On the one hand, good works are not acceptable, but on the other, we are commanded to do good works. A preferable approach would show that God's grace and love leads me to share the same with others. Although he rejected an imitation of Christ (because Christ's vocation is unique), he nevertheless concludes his work with the admonition, "be ye therefore imitators. . . ." [65]

In summary, *The Cost of Discipleship* remains an important work. As Christendom heads into the turbulent 70s, the call for costly grace appears more needed than ever. The student rebellion is directed in part at the failure of the older generation to take seriously the values it presumably espouses. The contemporary criticism of the church is related to merchandising in cheap grace where the church has not loved *all* men equally, has not preached the need for repentance from all sin, and has not forsaken the world for the service of Christ. A decade or two from now *The Cost of Discipleship* may stand out as Bonhoeffer's most important word to us.

VII. The Church
Confronting the World

Bonhoeffer's last book was his *Ethics*. Intended as lectures for Edinburgh, it was considered by Bonhoeffer as his lifework, his real contribution to theology, and was composed between 1940 and 1943. The work was uncompleted and some of the chapters break off abruptly. However, it is a work of great significance, termed by some as his most significant.[1] The book has been arranged in its present order by Eberhard Bethge.

THE UNIQUENESS OF CHRISTIAN ETHICS

The first chapter is foundational. It poses a chasm between Christian ethics and other ethical systems. Other ethical systems aim at coming to a knowledge of good and evil but say nothing about why this should be a particular emphasis in ethics. Christian ethics has a knowledge of why other ethical systems concentrate on the knowledge of good and evil, but rejects this goal as being a false one. The goal of Christian ethics is the new man, the restored man, the reconciled man, the man in God. When other ethical systems set up the goal of a knowledge of good and evil, man immediately becomes the arbiter of that knowledge and assumes the role of God who alone has this knowledge. "Instead of knowing only the God who is good to him and instead of knowing all things in Him, he now knows himself as the origin of good and evil."[2]

The man's rebellion brings disunion with God, with man, and within himself. The disunion is manifest in shame. Shame is man's ineffaceable recollection of his estrangement from the origin.[3] Because of it he needs a mask. It reflects man's disunion with God and with others, whereas conscience "is the sign of man's disunion with himself."[4] Although conscience may pretend to be many things, even the voice of God, it is limited in its functional relationship of judging what has been done in the way of wrong. It holds no positive command.

Bonhoeffer treats the Pharisee as the example of disunited man interested in the knowledge of right and wrong, often in a legalistic sense, but who, because of this question, never saw the real issue at hand: unity with God. Passing judgment on the actions of others became the Pharisee's favorite pastime, and brought disunion. Thus the demand of Jesus is to overcome the knowledge of good and evil for the union with God that brings union within man and among men. "No longer knowing good and evil, but knowing Christ as origin and as reconciliation, man will know all."[5] The teachings of Jesus forbid man to "know" or approve of his own actions, or his own goodness. Although this is psychologically impossible as far as knowledge or epistemology[6] goes, it is religiously possible in knowing one's reconciliation with God. Thus the religious life is not a matter of rules, "but solely of the living will of God."[7] Man's chief concern in all situations is to discern what God's will is. This must continue through life. Bonhoeffer does not imply direct inspiration of God's will, but he indicates that "if a man asks God humbly God will give him certain knowledge of His will."[8]

Accepting the given of the known will of God, what shall be the response? Intellectual acceptance? Reflective evaluation? No, the will of God is for *doing*. In the power of Jesus Christ man is to *do* the will of God. Bonhoeffer warns against a false doing of the will of God as well as a false hearing. This occurs when one does the law and his motive springs from his knowledge of good and evil rather than his union with God.

Man in union with God is marked by the stamp of love. Love takes its definition from the person Jesus Christ. "Love is the reconciliation of man with God in Jesus Christ." [9] In the act of reconciliation man is brought to unity, to union with God, and his relation to his neighbor is transformed. In unity his splitness is overcome.

The development of Bonhoeffer's thought at this point is cut off by an unfinished chapter. Thus we turn to the next which is also unfinished.

In "The Church and the World" Bonhoeffer got no further than eight pages, but two important and related ideas are set forth. The first concerns the non-Christian defense of an appeal to human values—such as reason, justice, culture—by those who share these values with the Christian but are not related to Christ. Bonhoeffer maintains that these values are homeless orphans who, in the hour of real danger, return to their real father. Jesus Christ is the origin of these values and "it is only under His protection" that they can survive. [10] The justification of these values is related to him alone. The second concern is that of Christ and good people. Too little has been said about the good man in Christianity. Much has been preached about the bad. Bonhoeffer declares that Christ belongs to both. Bonhoeffer felt that a theology of the good man should be further developed. A note showing the incompleteness of the chapter indicated something of his feeling: " 'I feel about it more or less like this: the good citizen, too, is humble before God, but the vicious man really lives only by grace.' " [11] It is regrettable that this thought was not developed further.

The third essay is on ethics as formation. Bonhoeffer assesses the various theoretical possibilities for solving the ethical dilemmas: *reason* (it fails to see "the depths of evil or the depths of the holy") ; *fanaticism* (it loses sight of the totality

of evil in concentrating upon a particular evil); *conscience*
(it becomes timid and uncertain because of the disguises of
evil and degenerates to a soothed conscience to avoid despair); *duty* (commanded duty does not have the free responsibility of the doer back of it); *freedom* (it often involves one
in doing bad to ward off a worse event); *private virtuousness*
(one must remain blind to evils around him and be self-
deceived).[12]

These options may have been useful in past days, but new
weapons are needed today. The answer Bonhoeffer proposes
is the will of God. The will of God is completely exposed in
Jesus Christ; it becomes near and personal in him. The wise
man is one who sees beyond principles, rules, and other
screens to the reality of God. In Jesus Christ the world is
reconciled, not overthrown. In the Incarnation where God
becomes man, God wishes for man to become true man, for
Jesus is not merely a man, but is *man*.

The fact of reconciliation poses problems for the world
especially when it views life from the standpoint of success.
Success covers the multitude of sins and guilt. Bonhoeffer
poses three attitudes toward success: (1) it is identified with
good; (2) "only good is successful"; (3) "all success comes
of wickedness."[13] Jesus Christ stands as a rejection of success
as the standard. Success or failure mean nothing in place of
"willing acceptance of God's judgment."[14]

The concern of the Christian is with conformation—the
forming of Christ in the believer—not with programs, plans,
and the practical as opposed to doctrinal concerns. Conformation is achieved by Christ, not by "efforts 'to become like
Jesus.' "[15] Bonhoeffer's perennial theme of the church being
Christ incarnate is renewed here. The church is where Christ
takes form. This keeps the church from being merely a religious organization, although the church may be tempted to
lapse in this direction.

Thus, the beginning point of Christian ethics is not rules

but the form of Christ and "formation of the Church in conformity with the form of Christ." [16] Thus there is no abstract ethic for all practices, but rather the question of whether "my action is at this moment helping my neighbour to become a man before God." [17] In this Christ affirms reality. Christian ethics becomes concerned with the concrete rather than the abstract, the universal principle. Christ becomes man, not a universal principle. Ethics is also beyond casuistry which becomes unmanageable. Reconciliation makes possible the existence of man as real man. Christian ethics begins with this departure point: how can Christ be formed in our world?

To give a background of the problem of forming Christ in the world, Bonhoeffer analyzes the historical antecedents of present secular trends. The breakup of Christian unity in the Reformation paved the way for the emancipation of reason and its deification. Science, once subservient, now assumes mastery over nature. Technology must be acknowledged as a heritage of Western history, and modern man has the problem of coming to grips with it rather than turning backwards to pretechnical times. Following the emancipation of reason came "the discovery of the Rights of Man." [18] Attention is focused on the masses who have "now come of age." [19] This in turn is related to nationalism. Bonhoeffer sees in the French Revolution the results of these movements. The machine becomes man's enemy, freedom and the rights of the masses lead to the guillotine, and nationalism engenders war. Nihilism stands at the end. Two things stand against the "plunge into the void": (1) a renewal of faith and (2) the "restrainer" (see 2 Thess. 2:7), which is the state's order and power.[20] The church's work is to prove to its worldly witnesses that its Lord is living.

Bonhoeffer's solution involves a turning back. For technology, nationalism, and reason, there is no turning back to a prestate of things. But there is a turning back by recognizing "the guilt incurred towards Christ." [21] Only in turning to

Christ will man turn to his true self. The church is the place
where the recognition of guilt takes place. Unlike the moral-
ist, however, there is no searching for the guilty party, but
only receiving forgiveness for the guilt. Bonhoeffer's list of
confessed faults touches upon the problems of our age and all
ages.[22]

If the church would be transformed and have Christ formed
in her, she must confess or lose her nature as the church of
Christ. The renewal of the church is linked with the renewal
of the Western world. Forgiveness, not the law of retribution,
must be at work among the nations. The church holds the key
to this in its confession of guilt.

Essay four is entitled, "The Last Things and the Things
Before the Last," or put more briefly, the ultimate and the
penultimate. The ultimate word, or last word, is that of
justification by faith alone. Man stands before God in Christ
on this basis, and only on this basis. Therefore religious
methods, ethical rightness, and civic achievement are rejected as the foundation of right-standing in God's presence.
If justification by faith is the last word, does this mean that
we must flee the world and radically reject it? Are we to live
only by the ultimate? What is the place of the penultimate?
What of our existence in the world as it stands before God?
The seeming alternative to radical rejection of the world is
acceptance of it as a compromise position implying rejection
of the ultimate. The two positions stand in opposition to one
another.

Bonhoeffer finds the solution in Jesus Christ. The Incarnation shows God's love for his work, the crucifixion shows
his judgment upon the creature, and the resurrection indicates a new world to come. God's becoming man means that
man is called to be man, to be himself, a penultimate in the
light of the ultimate. The cross shows the penultimate nature
of the world, meaning that man is not to be deified but to live
before the judgment of the final. The resurrection does not

annul life but makes it greater in the ultimate. Thus, "Christian life is participation in the encounter of Christ with the world." [23]

The penultimate is functional, the ultimate is the goal. The ultimate justifies the penultimate in its existence, but not as something independent of the ultimate. The penultimate prepares the way for coming to Christ. Without the ultimate the penultimate will shatter. Bonhoeffer analyzes Western Christendom from this perspective. In the last two centuries the ultimate has been called into question and the penultimate—peace, order, justice, humanness—breaks down. If the penultimate is to be fortified and strengthened, then there "must be a more emphatic proclamation of the ultimate." [24]

The penultimate concerns the natural as opposed to the supernatural. Bonhoeffer laments that the "natural" has been deleted from Protestantism because it has been opposed to grace, which is magnified. The natural is not the opposite of grace but of the unnatural. He argues that the gospel gives the basis for a recovery in Protestantism of the concept of the natural. [25] The natural, after the Fall, directs man toward Christ; the unnatural directs him away from Christ. The natural is unorganized; it is simply there; the unnatural consists of organization and therefore perverts the natural. The natural is recognized by reason. Its content is the preservation of life. Although one might rebel against the natural, the natural will endure in the long run for it preserves life.

Bonhoeffer rejects natural life as an end in itself (vitalism) and life as a means to an end (mechanization) for a composite view of life as both an end and a means. In the first there is content for creaturehood, and in the second, participation in the kingdom of God. Related to life are rights and duties in that order. "God gives before He demands." The general formulation of rights is found in the principle "*suum cuique,* to each his own." [26] Both the multiplicity and unity of rights are expressed in this principle. Bonhoeffer sees God as the defender of natural rights.

ETHICAL ISSUES

In application Bonhoeffer considers certain issues in the framework of natural rights. The first is bodily life which is innate; that is, we exist without a choice or will. Since there is life, and since at death all rights cease, the conclusion is reached that natural life should be free of "intentional injury, violation and killing." [27] Because bodiliness is an end in itself, bodily joys can be justified; but being also a means, the body must not be content with pleasures alone.

In this section Bonhoeffer declares that because man's life exists, he has a natural right to live. No one then has the right to take life arbitrarily. Euthanasia is morally wrong because it involves the arbitrary killing of innocent life. On the other hand, war is defended by Bonhoeffer because it is *not* arbitrary killing. War is more complex, because the soldier may be personally innocent but collectively guilty in a military attack upon a country.

Bonhoeffer argues for these and other positions below on the basis of a natural-life motif intermingled with Scripture proof. One might question why both are used. Why not divine revelation alone? Or, natural law alone? Both are used because he holds that God stands back of the natural and gives it meaning, while at the same time revelation is necessary for a precise understanding of God's will.

He is weaker in dealing with suicide. Man differs from other creatures in that he can freely take his life. In suicide he attempts "to give a final human meaning to a life which has become humanly meaningless." [28] Bonhoeffer's ground for declaring it wrong is not so much natural law as the fact of incurring God's judgment of guilt. Suicide shows a lack of faith in God and in life's possibilities.

Leading up to the issues of birth control and abortion he declares that marriage is a natural right of man rather than a religious or civil institution. It existed from the beginning of man before the development of these institutions. Marriage naturally includes the right of life to come into being. When conception has taken place, an abortive act is simply murder.[29] Likewise birth control practiced perpetually as excluding life is a serious violation of man's natural existence. Bonhoeffer hedges on sterilization when either intense passion is involved or disease, in which cases it might be medically necessary.

The last issue is bodily freedom which prohibits rape, slavery, and torture. Bonhoeffer began a section on the natural rights of the life of the mind, but this was left unfinished. A note left something of the outline to be followed which included a section on culture. It is regretted that we are bereft of this material.

WHAT IT MEANS TO BE REAL

The next essay, "Christ, Reality, and Good," is a further treatment in depth of the view that Christian ethics is not concerned with the knowledge of good and evil. He declares that the questions "How can I be good?" and "How can I do good?" are supplanted by a different question: "What is the will of God?" [30] The first two questions reduce the idea of good to an abstraction. Bonhoeffer's question concerns ultimate reality, and although he presupposes faith, it makes ethics concrete and specific. The ultimate reality is seen in none other than Jesus Christ who is not an idea of good, or an abstraction. Consequently that aspect of ethical discourses given over to the question of motives and consequences not only divides man up in an arbitrary way but does not reflect the real, or God's self-revelation. The real purpose of ethics is to participate in reality. In Christ this becomes actual.

If there is one ultimate reality, why do we think in terms of two spheres of nature and grace, sacred and profane, and other opposites? Bonhoeffer rejects the two antinomies because there is only one reality, God, who has become manifest in Christ and in the world.[31] These antinomies that are reflected in Roman Catholic as well as post-Reformation thought are nonbiblical. There is no possibility of being a Christian outside of the world or outside of Christ. Even the kingdom of the devil does not support the two spheres, for "he must serve Christ even against his will." [32] The world has been reconciled in Christ. To accept the two spheres is to neglect or reject this reconciliation.

Although the world may not recognize or acknowledge it, the world is related to Christ in the mandates of God: labor, marriage, government, and the church.[33] The "word mandate refers more clearly to a divinely imposed task rather than to a determination of being." [34] The mandates are divine because of origin rather than in their nature as such. The realm of government attracts attention because Bonhoeffer was struggling with the Nazi encroachment in all areas of life. Government is not creative, but preserves and protects what is already created—that is, labor and marriage.

Obedience is owed the government because of Christ's command. This is an implication of the mandate. But is there an exception to this command? How does Bonhoeffer harmonize obedience to the government with his involvement in an assassination plot? The exceptional situation of tyranny calling for an assassination attempt is not dealt with in a theoretical way by Bonhoeffer. The mandates provide *normative* rather than exceptional or extraordinary directions for the will of God, the base of the Christian ethic. In fulfilling all the mandates, one participates in reality.

The next essay, "History and Good," builds the concept of responsibility around the biblical self-assertion of Christ: "I am the Life." Life is a Who, not a What. True responsibility is the pledge of one's life in a life and death way. Responsibility is "to and for God, to men and for men . . . for the sake of Jesus Christ." [35] Responsibility rests both upon freedom and upon being bound to man and to God. Responsibility is also defined as "deputyship," acting in behalf of others. In Jesus, deputyship is assumed for the whole of humanity. For man, deputyship involves "surrender of one's own life to the other man." [36] Thus "only the selfless man lives." [37]

Responsibility is limited by the other man, who is also a responsible creature. Responsibility cannot be used to coerce another person to action. It is also limited in application. It does not lead to revolutionary action but to doing "what is necessary at the given place and with a due consideration of reality." [38] The *direction* that responsibility dictates depends upon the situation. Bonhoeffer gives us a situation ethic bound to reality (which is Christ); i.e., act in accordance with Christ. [39] He rejects an absolute rule or law which must be imposed upon every situation. The so-called absolute good may be the very worst action possible. Action can be directed by the word of Jesus which is the interpretation of his life. Since Christ is no stranger to human reality, there is no arbitrary division between secular and Christian principles. Reality has been reconciled in Christ. To follow him is to have a meaningful word concerning actions in reality.

Although responsibility is a relation between persons, Bonhoeffer speaks of pertinence, the relation that man has with the world of things. [40] First, one must keep in mind the divine origin of things. Things are for use. Second, each thing has "its own law of being." [41] Man must learn these laws, and responsible action means that he abides by the inherent laws of things, whether it be the state, the corporation, or human growth. The exception to the rule, the situation, is granted in the case of the *necessità*, the action required which cannot be made on the basis of the law of the being. War, for instance, would be the exception in the political area, or the necessity. But whether one abides by the law of the being or in freedom does the expedient, both actions stand before God who judges them. Guilt may be accepted in the knowledge that it can be forgiven.

If there is guilt, what of the conscience? Conscience will not permit one to take blame for the sake of another. The reason is that conscience seeks a unity with itself. With a loss of unity conscience indicts the self. The unity, in part, arises out of the ego's desire to justify its action before God. Bonhoeffer's answer to the divided conscience is self-denial and commitment to Jesus Christ who becomes "my conscience." [42] In the surrender of the ego to God, conscience is set free from the law for a greater foundation—mercy in Jesus Christ. Thus Bonhoeffer could justify telling a lie to a murderer who asks if a pursued man is in his house. Reality and responsibility demand such. But the guilt of conscience will be found innocent in Christ in this action. In Christ, the conscience finds that the law is not the last word.

To offend the conscience and to have responsibility, there must be freedom. The freedom that one has may seem questionable in light of environment, law, culture, routine, and other factors, but Bonhoeffer insists that freedom and responsibility prevail "in the encounter with other people." [43] Freedom and responsibility are not isolated from but are related to obedience. "Obedience without freedom is slavery; freedom without obedience is arbitrary self-will. Obedience restrains freedom; and freedom ennobles obedience." [44]

Where is the place of responsibility, freedom, and obedience? Rejecting the pseudo-Lutheran view which attempted to justify existence in this world as only being on a pilgrimage, Bonhoeffer now declares that a man "takes up his position against the world *in* the world; the calling is the place at which the call of Christ is answered, the place at which a man lives responsibly." [45] "Vocation is responsibility and responsibility is a total response of the whole man to the whole of reality." [46] Thus he declares that a pastor must be concerned for the whole church rather than merely for his own isolated flock. When a minister refused to raise his voice in the church struggle against the Nazis to defend other congregations, or to protest persecutions outside his congregation, his own flock was eventually lost.

Bonhoeffer is putting forth a form of situationalism. One may have to break the law in order that the law be meaningfully fulfilled. War involves many subterfuges that peace, honesty, and integrity might prevail. But it is not an extreme form of situationalism that glosses over the means to achieving a worthy end. Even the means must be repented of, given the situation. This section was to be continued and an outline was preserved, but Bonhoeffer was never able to return to it.

THE MANDATES

The seventh essay, "The 'Ethical' and the 'Christian' as a Theme," touches on the matter of authority for decision-making. Can one construct an ethical system applicable to all times and places? Are our decisions always of a moral nature, demanding a decision between right and wrong? Bonhoeffer answers that the ethic is not a book, a universal reference for all actions without exception. Neither can there be an ethicist who performs the same function. Indeed, ethical discourse is related to the concrete, the specific, the event in time and place. By the same token, one cannot take a positivistic view of ethical discourse and admit only that reality furnishes nothing beyond itself. The parallel situation is the position of a teaching church which demands submission to its precepts. This Bonhoeffer regards as substituting a religious positivism for an empirical positivism.

To avoid these opposites he proposes the "Commandment of God," which is "the total and concrete claim laid to man by the merciful and holy God in Jesus Christ." [47] Embracing all of life it sets free as well as binds, but it is not a summary of all ethical principles to be applied by the individual. If the interpretation or application of the commandment is left to the individual it is no longer *God's* commandment.

A commandment must be as concrete as life and as up-to-date as man's life. Does God give specific directions by new revelations for each occasion? No, but God does confront man in the present historical situation by his command. In a concrete way God's commandment in Christ comes to us "in the Church, in the family, in labour and in government." [48]

The mandates embrace the whole of life. In them God has already commanded styles of living wherein there is freedom "from the anxiety and the uncertainty of decision." [49] Mandates are different from ethical precepts, for the latter concentrate upon what is not permitted while mandates give positive instruction for the content of life. He asserts that in the mandates "life flows freely. It lets man eat, drink, sleep, work, rest and play. It does not interrupt him. It does not continually ask whether he ought to be sleeping, eating, working, or playing, or whether he has some more urgent duties." [50]

Mandate is defined as "the concrete divine commission which has its foundation in the revelation of Christ and which is evidenced by Scripture; it is the legitimation and warrant for the execution of a definite divine commandment." [51] He rejects the use of the terms "institution" (which implies divine sanction for any status quo), "estate" (too many new connotations which distort the original Reformation usage), and "office" (it is now secularized and associated with bureaucracy). He prefers the term "mandate" to express some of the original meanings of the rejected words. The commandment of God in Christ serves as the basis for the mandates. They are not the result of historical development, but are imposed from above. As a further line of explanation the mandates are "conjoined" with one another. No mandate has independence over the others.

Although the chapter is incomplete there is some treatment of the commandment of God in the church with reference to the other spheres, or mandates. Preaching and confession both express the commandment of God in the church. To stress one of these without the other is to deprive the church of a concrete ethic. The Protestant Church stresses preaching while the Roman Church stresses confession, or church worship. The Reformed Church is poverty-stricken in worship, liturgy, spiritual exercises, and discipline, while the Roman Church has neglected the proclamation of the Scripture.[52]

The church has a word for all of society, a single word of proclamation for both believer and unbeliever alike. This word is summed up in three phrases: (1) *"Jesus Christ, the eternal Son with the Father for all eternity."* This means that nothing exists apart from God, and that no created thing can be understood apart from Christ. The Incarnation means that God can now be found in human form, and therefore man is free to be man before God. Thus a "genuine worldliness" now becomes a possibility. (2) *"Jesus Christ, the Crucified Reconciler."* The cross sets us free from trying to deify the world, and calls us to believe that the world is already reconciled to God. Therefore it is possible to live a life in genuine worldliness, by allowing the world to be what it is before God. (3) *"Jesus Christ, the risen and ascended Lord."* This means that Jesus Christ is Creator, Reconciler, and Redeemer. A Christonomy, a rule of Christ, replaces heteronomy and autonomy. Although Christ rules the church, the church does not rule the world. She never ceases being the church, but she cannot be more.[53]

A MISCELLANY OF ESSAYS

Part Two of *Ethics* contains an assortment of essays. The first has the formidable title, "The Doctrine of the Primus Usus Legis According to the Lutheran Symbolic Writings." Two basic issues are brought up: what is the relation of the law to the gospel, and what is the relation of the decalogue to natural law. Lutheran usage suggested that the primary use of the law relates to works, the secondary to the knowledge of sin, and the third to the fulfillment of the law and forgiveness. Bonhoeffer maintains that all three are included in proclamation. He identifies the decalogue with natural law known by reason. There cannot be a dichotomy between the decalogue and natural law. Similarly, there cannot be an arbitrary division between the law and the gospel.[54] He notes, "There can be no Christian preaching of works without the preaching of the acknowledgment of sin and of the fulfilment of the law. And the law cannot be preached without the gospel." [55]

The second essay is on "Personal" and "Real" ethos. Bonhoeffer protests against the ethic of Dilschneider, Troeltsch, and Naumann, who regarded the Christian ethic as having little or nothing to say about the world's institutional structures, i.e., state, economics, and science. For them the religious ethic was reduced to the practice of love within the world's structures without having a mission of correction, improvement, and criticism of them. If their view is correct, Christian ethics would affect only about 10 percent of life. Bonhoeffer rejects these views because Christ created all things (including man, state, economy, nature, etc.), has reconciled all things, and the church is placed in the midst of the world where this message may be heard.

The rule of Christ makes it now possible for a genuine world order in these spheres to come about. True worldliness means that these institutions should become what they were meant to be in obedience to God. The state should actually be the state; it is not to rule over the church or be subject to the church or to any other alien law.

Bonhoeffer rejects the three estates of Lutheran doctrine (economic, political, and ecclesiastical) for the biblical mandates which have a heavenly archetype: marriage (Christ and the church), labor (the creative work of God in the world), government (the dominion of Christ in eternity), and the state (the city of God). He defends his position against the charge that the secular institutions are able to survive without knowing Christ. Limitations are placed on this claim, for "genuine worldliness is achieved only through emancipation by Christ," and yet they exist only because of Christ whether this is known or not.[56]

The third essay is entitled "State and Church." Bonhoeffer avers that the concept of the state is pagan in origin and is alien to the New Testament. Government is the New Testament idea which does not imply any particular form of state or society. Government is ordained by God. Bonhoeffer rejects those bases for government which project the state arising out of the character of man: i.e., Aristotle, medieval Catholicism, Hegelianism; as well as those theories based in man's sin and need of government for restraint in a chaotic world: i.e., the Reformation tradition. The second view is more biblical, affirming that government is "from above" rather than organized "from below." But in opposition to this Bonhoeffer affirms Christ as the basis for government because he is the mediator of creation, the goal of government, its Lord, and its source of authority and power.[57]

Government has a divine character in its *being*. This refers not to its origin, but to its nature. Its task reflects its divine character in its mission whereby it serves Christ by the sword for punishment and justice and along with education for goodness.[58] A further divine implication is the claim of government on conscience, or obedience "for the Lord's sake" (1 Pet. 2:13). The believer is bound to obedience until the government exceeds its commission, whereupon one must obey God rather than man. This disobedience in a single area must not be generalized to all areas of government. Only an apocalyptic event in which all obedience to government involved denial of Christ (see Rev. 13:7) would require total disobedience.[59]

Government has a relation to the other mandates. It serves to protect and sanction these areas, but in itself government is not creative. Marriage, labor, and the church stand independently of government, but always in the presence of government and subject to its supervision for the sake of order.

Government has a claim on the church in obedience. Obedience to government is obedience to Christ. Likewise, the church lays a claim on government. She reminds government of their common Master. She calls government to fulfill its "worldly calling," its special task, and at the same time claims protection from the government. The government also has a claim on the church. Government must maintain neutrality with reference to exalting one religion over another. It cannot originate new religions. Similarly, the church has a political responsibility. The church must warn of sin and call for righteousness which exalts a nation.

Bonhoeffer does not opt for any particular form of government. Any form that best fulfills the nature of government would be accepted. This means that government must recognize its being from above. It means also that the government's power will rest on a strict execution of justice, on the rights of the family and of labor, and on the proclamation of the gospel.[60]

Essay four, "On the Possibility of the Word of the Church to the World," is unfinished but it poses the issue of the church's responsibility for answering particular problems in the world. Does the church have an answer for all the ills of mankind? Bonhoeffer remarks that Jesus hardly discussed such solutions, but stressed the redemption of man. Therefore, he suggests, "perhaps the unsolved state of these problems is of more importance to God than their solution, for it may serve to call attention to the fall of man and to the divine redemption."[61] The solution of human problems is not the task of the church. The church does have a responsibility in removing hindrances to man's coming to faith in Christ. This is a negative responsibility in which she declares the wrongness of an economic theory, for example, if it obstructs belief in Christ. Positively, she can give advice by drawing upon specialists. This latter task is a service, not part of her divine office.

Essay five, "What Is Meant by 'Telling the Truth?' " concludes the *Ethics*. Truthfulness, Bonhoeffer says, does not mean blurting out everything one knows to anybody one meets. Telling the truth depends on the occasion, who is addressing me, and on the subject under discussion. It must involve the total reality of the situation. A true word spoken hypocritically is really untrue. Man is not entitled to speak his mind on any subject apart from the need or demand for his thoughts. On the other hand, "the right to speak always lies within the confines of the particular office which I discharge" [62]—as parent or teacher, for instance. Of interest is the editor's footnote quoting Bonhoeffer's letter of December 1943. He speaks of the need for concealment—e.g., God made clothes for man in a fallen state—in which, although evil cannot be eradicated, "it is at least to be kept hidden." [63] If there is to be confession, let it be before God. This may serve as a needed corrective to the bent toward spiritual stripteases that occur in sensitivity groups and related psychologically oriented movements in evangelical Christianity.

Trying to evaluate an unfinished work and being fair in doing it is impossible. What one might criticize would conceivably have no basis had Bonhoeffer finished the work, polished and revised it. Yet in spite of the unfinished nature of the work we add the following comments and questions. First, the title, *Ethics*, is perhaps a misnomer. Suggested titles could be *Christian Ethics*, *Theological Ethics*, or *The Church and the World*. These would indicate the direction the work takes more than *Ethics*, because traditional approaches of philosophical ethics are rejected as unreal from the beginning.

Second, Bonhoeffer insists that ethics must be defined concretely. God's will must be seen in a definite way as it is declared in the mandates of labor, marriage, government, and the church. Bonhoeffer saw the mandates as giving man freedom to live without having constantly to reflect on issues to be decided and thereby being kept in a state of indecision. But the mandates do not go far enough. Even with the mandates many Christians may still be troubled. They want to know the specific answer to concrete questions: Whom shall I marry? How can I do God's will in this particular choice? How many children shall I have? Under the mandate of labor, what specific calling shall I follow? To my knowledge Bonhoeffer leaves us without answers. But these are serious questions facing young Christians, and all discerning people who contemplate their future.

Third, there appears to be an antinomy between the church's role in prohibiting tyranny and the church's inability to give "Christian answers" to secular problems. Bonhoeffer advocated reshaping society to prevent tyranny even if it meant assassination. (Admittedly, he wanted to dissociate himself from the Confessing Church had the assassination attempt on Hitler been successful, but this is not the usual advice given as the content of Christian ethics.) On the other hand, in admitting that the world's problems may be insoluble Bonhoeffer sides with inaction and the status quo. The word that God has for man, he says, is redemption, not solution.

This antinomy exists and has existed in the church for a long time. What would Bonhoeffer have said about the civil rights movement? Should the church be involved in helping a depressed people? How would Bonhoeffer express himself on the Vietnam issue, or the threat of Communism as a form of tyranny? What areas in the world are open for "reshaping," or what areas are "insoluble"? These and similar questions would no doubt have received creative answers had Bonhoeffer lived to face them in their exact form.

Fourth, Bonhoeffer's situational ethic is better than some contemporary writers', but there are still questions to be asked. His is better in that it is dictated by the "form of Christ, and its taking form amidst a band of men." [64] Some contemporary writers speak of the end sanctifying the means, giving considerable laxity to ethical application. Bonhoeffer does not do this, but the difference may be little more than verbal. He declares that "Christ teaches no abstract ethics such as must at all cost be put into practice." [65] But what is the "form of Christ"? How is it to be known except through the gospel's declaring redemption and the development of a life style centered around the teaching of the New Testament? Can ethics be built upon the unusual, the extraordinary, the purely situational, or the so-called "hard cases" of life? Must not the form of Christ begin with the specific and add an addenda for the unusual only when necessary, and even then only in repentance?

In summary, Bonhoeffer's *Ethics* was written for a crisis situation. He was concerned that tyranny not arise again. He was disturbed over the silence and apathy of the church during Hitler's rise. His situationalism is in part to be understood in this context. One must not tell the truth to a tyrant when harm will come to good people. While situationalism appears attractive, it is not easy. The situations change, the issues are not always the same, and human judgment falters. While Christ "affirms reality," [66] the moral instruction in the New Testament gives content to that reality.

Ethics will rank as one of Bonhoeffer's greatest works, although it will not hold the fascination of the last volume, which contains his letters from prison. To that we now turn.

VIII. The Church Against Religion

The book that made Bonhoeffer a question mark to many minds was *Letters and Papers from Prison.*[1] Those provocative phrases like "religionless Christianity," "the God who forsakes us," "Jesus as the man for others," and similar phrases appear in context that are only in outline form without full contextual meanings. This is the work that has captivated the interests of diverse theologians who quote it in bolstering their own theological stance.

Will we ever understand the "later" Bonhoeffer? Can we hope to when we have received only tenuous expressions? Are we justified in taking a few personal letters and basing a new imposing theological structure on them? These are some of the problems and implications of the last words of Bonhoeffer. This work is also difficult to treat because of its miscellaneous nature. At best we can only hope to treat some of the rich themes found herein.

The first piece is an essay composed around 1942–43, prior to his arrest, entitled "After Ten Years." It begins with a treatment of the intolerable times during which people had lost their moorings. Evil appeared in the guise of light and all traditional ethical concepts were thrown into conflict. Bonhoeffer discusses the reactions of reasonable people (who are disappointed by the unreasonableness of both sides in the world's conflicts); conscience-guided people (who are deceived by the seductive disguises of evil and accept a salved rather than clear conscience); moral fanatics (who get trapped in nonessentials); duty-guided people (who never achieve a direct hit on evil); the person claiming freedom (who performs evil to ward off a greater evil); and the man of private virtuousness (who plays the game of self-deception or becomes a great hypocrite).[2] Is there a better answer? Who can stand fast? Only the man who sacrifices all in "exclusive allegiance to God." "Where are such people?" Bonhoeffer asks.

People of civil courage were lacking, for the Germans had learned the virtue of obedience. But submissiveness can be exploited, and in the case of Nazi Germany it was. Responsibility is related to free men. Obedience goes only so far. Bonhoeffer then turns to various categories of relationships and attitudes.

1. *Success.* Success achieved by good means can be overlooked ethically, but success by means of evil poses problems. Success tends to make good out of evil in history. Bonhoeffer regarded himself as responsibly involved in learning how the coming generation is to live in a new culture.

2. *Folly.* Bonhoeffer regards folly as more devastating than evil. There is no reasoning with, protesting against, or upending the fool. He calls folly a sociological problem, called forth by violent displays of power which deprive men of their judgment. The only hope against folly is liberation, and the ultimate release is a responsible life before God. In the political arena, "what will really matter is whether those in power expect more from people's folly than from their wisdom and independence of mind."[3]

3. *Contempt for humanity* will be rejected only if we realize that what we despise in others is never "entirely absent from ourselves."[4]

4. *Immanent righteousness.* Bonhoeffer says that evil carries the seeds of its own destruction. The world seems ordered

in a way that the expedient act cannot be turned into a principle without suffering retribution. This affirmation leads Bonhoeffer to set forth some statements of faith on the sovereignty of God in history. God can bring good out of evil, and gives strength in times of distress. He hears our prayers and desires responsible action from us.

5. *Confidence.* Bonhoeffer writes that although betrayal is everywhere, trust and confidence are greater than ever imagined. In trust they placed their lives in the hands of others. Such trust is a rare blessing and a necessity against the background of mistrust in society.

6. *The sense of quality.* He takes a new look at equalitarian movements which destroy a sense of quality by destroying reserve. Socially this means a break with the "cult of the star" tradition in society and culturally it substitutes the book for the newspaper, leisure for frenzied activity, quality for quantity.

7. *Sympathy.* Bonhoeffer declares that sympathy arises with the imminence of danger. Christians are called to sympathy and action when others are in danger.

8. *Suffering.* In the past one could plan both his professional and his private life. But war makes both of these impossible. Life must be carried on living every day as if it is our last, and yet in faith and responsibility as though there is to be a great future. This is still a germane principle today.

9. *Optimism.* Pessimism is wiser than optimism, but optimism must not be impugned even though it is proven wrong many times. Optimism—in spite of the day of judgment—leads to building and hoping for a better world.

10. *Insecurity and death.* Both had been increasingly in Bonhoeffer's mind as these ten years passed by. By accepting death, each new day of life becomes miraculous. His own death is prefigured in this descriptive statement: "It is we ourselves, and not outward circumstances, who make death what it can be, a death freely and voluntarily accepted." [5]

The essay concludes with the question: "Are we still of any use?" Much evil has been devised and experienced. The need is for "plain, honest, straightforward men." Is it possible to regain this stance after the evils of intrigue, war, and cynicism? [6] Bonhoeffer does not answer his question.

The next section consists of Bonhoeffer's letters to his parents. In them we are shown the closeness of his family feeling rather than any profound theological views. Bonhoeffer read a great deal in prison. The subject matter was broad: newspapers, novels, history, philosophy, theology, music, and the Bible. He memorized verses of Scripture each day, especially psalms. Much of his reading was in nineteenth-century writing; he had great admiration for its literary output. The letters to his parents reflect his occasional sickness, the growing problem of food, his gradual callousness to prison life, and the irritating desire to get out and on with important things.

While in prison he had occasion to write a wedding sermon for his niece and his close friend, Eberhard Bethge. The "Wedding Sermon from a Prison Cell" progresses in five statements: "God is guiding your marriage"; "God makes your marriage indissoluble"; "God establishes a rule of life by which you can live together in wedlock" (Col. 3:18, 19); "God has laid on marriage a blessing and a burden," that of children; "God gives you Christ as the foundation of your marriage." [7] The sermon is characterized by a tenderness born of love for both participants in the wedding.

Letters and Papers from Prison also contains a report on prison life revealing the sadistic character of some of its guards, the injustice in treatment of prisoners, the inhumanity toward the less important prisoners, and the growing problem of food. The lack of air-raid protection was a prime source of anxiety for the 700 men in the prison. Bonhoeffer reflects on his embarrassment at preferred treatment when his position and family connections were learned.

The major part of *Letters and Papers from Prison* contains
letters written to a friend, Eberhard Bethge. This section contains the enigmatic phrases so prominent in Bonhoeffer devo-
tees. In dealing with them we are confronted with the issue of
interpretation. How much weight should be given to fragmen-
tary letters in which the author freely acknowledges that he
has not worked out his ideas?[8] Can Bonhoeffer's criticism of
religion mean that he was bordering on the loss of his faith?
Even if this were true, should one give heavy weight to utterances born out of the frustration of a Nazi prison? What is
to be made of these statements?

The following items seem to have provoked the most interest. First, *the problem of religion.* The letter of April 30,
1944, contains Bonhoeffer's confession of the radical emphasis that his thinking had taken. He wrote, "We are moving
towards a completely religionless time; people as they are
now simply cannot be religious any more."[9] Freedom from
religion is compared to freedom from the rite of circumcision
in the time of Paul the apostle. Religion is opposed to being
a Christian. Bonhoeffer regards Barth's criticism of religion
as his greatest contribution, although Barth does not go far
enough.

Religion uses God as the lazy way of explaining the unex-
plainable. God is on the edge of human boundaries. But what
happens when the human boundaries are pushed back and an
alternate explanation is given for the phenomena once cred-
ited to God? God is pushed further from human existence.[10]
Countering this, Bonhoeffer insists that God must be met in
the center of life rather than on the periphery. He must be
found in man's strength, not his weakness; in life's goodness,
not in death and guilt alone.[11] Bonhoeffer's question boils
down to this: If by science man solves the problems of hunger
and disease, if by education the problems of guilt, if by psychiatry the ills of the mind, if man's other needs can be met,
what room is left for God? Bonhoeffer rejects the "God of

the gaps" for the Incarnate Christ who is *in the world*, not as an idea, but as Person. "We are to find God in what we know, not in what we do not know; God wants us to realize his presence, not in unsolved problems but in those that are solved." [12]

Second, *the problem of the "world come of age."* This term relates to religion's use of the idea of God. Through science, man has discarded God's role in the universe. Questions can be answered "without recourse to the 'working hypothesis' called 'God.' " [13] Christian apologetics, however, has continued in its retreat, hoping to take refuge in "ultimate questions" such as death, guilt, and meaning in life. Thus religion's approach to man "come of age" has been to bring him to a sense of guilt and despair to make him sense his need for Christ. This "methodist" approach is labeled as pointless (it puts an adult back into adolescence), ignoble (it exploits man's weakness), and un-Christian ("it confuses Christ with one particular stage in man's religiousness"). [14]

If we cannot roll back the advances of science, the conclusions of philosophers, the desertion of religion by ethics and politics, where does this leave God? Bonhoeffer answers:

> So our coming of age leads us to a true recognition of our situation before God. God would have us know that we must live as men who manage our lives without him. The God who is with us is the God who forsakes us (Mark 15:34). The God who lets us live in the world without the working hypothesis of God is the God before whom we stand continually. Before God and with God we live without God. God lets himself be pushed out of the world on to the cross. [15]

To be of age is not to be without God. Dropping the religious context means that God as a hypothesis is substituted by living with God in a relationship. God the omnipotent is not known; God the Incarnate is known as he comes to us in his weakness and suffering.

Third, *the problem of Christian worldliness*—a seeming contradiction in terms according to traditional use—or secularism. Bonhoeffer defines "this-worldliness" as

> living unreservedly in life's duties, problems, successes and failures, experiences and perplexities. In so doing we throw ourselves completely into the arms of God, taking seriously, not our own sufferings, but those of God in the world—watching with Christ in Gethsemane. That I think is faith, that is *metanoia;* and that is how one becomes a man and a Christian (cf. Jer. 45!).[16]

Taking one's duties and sufferings seriously means that we must exist for others. Jesus is "the man for others," and this type of relationship holds true for Christians. Bonhoeffer partially questions the theme of *The Cost of Discipleship* when it involves trying to make something of oneself, a stereotyped saint, sinner, or churchman.[17] Instead, both the Christian and the church exist for others. The church's role is to "tell men of every calling what it means to live in Christ, to exist for others." [18]

Bonhoeffer's attitude toward worldliness seems to arise out of his interest in the thirteenth century.[19] Drawing upon his musical ability in counterpoint he described life as a polyphony in which earthly love is the counterpoint to the fixed melody of loving God with all one's heart. Polyphony may be something of a theodicy in which pain and joy are parts of the total life structure just as bass fulfills the symmetry demanded by the treble.[20]

Bonhoeffer's understanding of worldliness shows again in his discussion of the central emphasis in Christianity. There is real danger in calling Christianity a "redemption from cares, distress, fears, and longings, from sin and death, in a better world beyond the grave." [21] Christianity is this-worldly for it sends a "man back to his life on earth in a wholly new way . . . ." [22] Bonhoeffer believed that if the world come of age was to be won to Christ it must be encountered in its strength, not its weaknesses. [23]

In searching for meaning and application of his thought, Bonhoeffer plays down the traditional idea of repentance as a religious act, concerned with one's own needs, and stresses rather the positive side of "allowing oneself to be caught up into the way of Jesus Christ." [24] Traditional acts of repentance are deplored as mere religious method. In this context he declares that the godlessness of the world perhaps makes it closer to God. Then the thought breaks off. We question whether repentance can be written off so freely. True, its positive emphasis is more important, for repentance without faith would lead to self-inflicted despair. But Jesus began and ended his ministry, according to Luke's Gospel, with the message that man should repent.

Fourth, *the problem of the church in transition.* In May of 1944, Bonhoeffer wrote some thoughts on the baptism of Dietrich Wilhelm Rüdiger Bethge, his godson. [25] Although participating in a rite that was outdated as far as modernity would have it, Bonhoeffer speaks of the future church that will have changed greatly. Its language will be nonreligious "as was Jesus' language." [26] By August of 1944, he urged the church to "come out of its stagnation." [27] There must be genuine conversation between the church and the world. In this same letter he proposed an outline for a future book. Chapter three would urge the church to give its wealth away to the needy; clergy should live on free-will offerings or support themselves by secular work. The church's work is to explain what it means to live in Christ. It should have a courageous word against the vices of pride and encouragement for the elements of the good life. Unfortunately the proposed book was never completed.

What are we to make of the thoughts expressed so vividly

in these intimate letters to a friend? It would be unwise to be dogmatic. Can we say that Bonhoeffer qualifies his early works in which he speaks of the visible church as the body of Christ? Does his disappointment with the national church in Germany and then later the weaknesses of the Confessing Church force him to modify his idea of the church's form? Is there not really a trend toward a noninstitutional but more biblical concept of the church?

Rather than venture too far in a direction that is filled with uncertainty, we had best stop in our conjecture and perhaps plead for the same from others who would interpret these phrases with a content that Bonhoeffer never intended. We may conclude that whatever else one may think about Bonhoeffer, he advocated Christianity without religion but certainly not Christianity without God. The nearness of God Incarnate is apparent in his last words before death: "This is the end—for me the beginning of life." [28]

In our final assessment of Bonhoeffer we will try to fit *Letters and Papers from Prison* into the overall picture of the man and his influence on the contemporary theological mind. To that evaluation we now turn.

IX. The Significance
of Bonhoeffer

THE MAN

Difficulty surrounds the attempt to evaluate Bonhoeffer. His influence grows and students will continue to turn to him and find inspiration in his germinal thinking. That part of the revolution in theology due to his influence is still with us. But at this point in history we can draw some ideas together about the man's significance. Time will tell whether this particular assessment stands true or not.

A beginning point is the man himself. More attention has been paid to his thought and ideas rather than to the man. Perhaps interest in the man himself will heighten since the definitive work of Eberhard Bethge, *Dietrich Bonhoeffer*, is now available in English translation. Both Bethge's work, and the excellent biography by Mary Bosanquet, *The Life and Death of Dietrich Bonhoeffer*, give a clear vision of the man, his style of life, his activity, his hopes, fears, aspirations, faith, and loyalty to Jesus Christ. Bonhoeffer is an inspiring example of a committed Christian. He deserves to be enrolled among the greater adventurers of faith. From the first, he set his face against tyranny in Germany. He was among the first to raise his voice against the monstrous persecution of the Jews when they were forbidden to hold public office or to enter or remain in the ministry of the church. The frustrating

opposition to the political church in Germany, the clandestine
seminary life operated by the Confessing Church, the intrigue
and plotting designed to rid Germany of a demonic rule make
him a fascinating person.

A vivid contrast could be drawn between Bonhoeffer and
Sir Thomas More. Could Hollywood do with Bonhoeffer what
it did with More in *A Man for All Seasons?* More was a man
who stood by his principles in an issue unworthy of martyrdom, while Bonhoeffer stood to the death for a purpose worthy
of giving one's life—to rid a country of tyranny. With the English translation of Eberhard Bethge's definitive biography, the
story of Bonhoeffer the man should take on renewed interest.

Protestantism does not have its roll of canonical saints, but
Bonhoeffer deserves to be enrolled in the memory as a hero
of faith. Bonhoeffer has a modernity that past adventurers of
faith do not. We rationalize by saying that life in previous
generations and cultures may have been much easier. But here
within a technological culture saturated with militarism, hate,
and divided peoples is a man familiar with it all and who has
something to say about it.

The person of Bonhoeffer assumes an interest for us in contrast to the other great theologians of his time. Karl Barth,
Emil Brunner, and Rudolf Bultmann are interesting for their
theologies. We have not focused any great attention upon
their personal lives. If we dismiss them for their theology or
accept them for it, we are not drawn to them as persons. With
Bonhoeffer it is different. We may also say that many other
pastors died in prison in Germany during the church struggle, but we have not been caught up with them. Bonhoeffer is
different. He is a rare soul who had many interests, a rare
being who came to grips with theology, and the kind of person who would die for his convictions. In an often used word
of this generation we could say that Bonhoeffer had *charisma.*
We are drawn to him, his person, and we want to know something of him as well as his theology.

THE THEOLOGICAL REVOLUTION

Bonhoeffer is important for his contribution to theology in general. Some new moods in theology that appeared in the early sixties appealed to Bonhoeffer's later works, particularly the *Letters and Papers from Prison*. The work of Bishop John A. T. Robinson made use of Bonhoeffer's terminology. The upheaval in theology following Robinson was notoriously journalistic, if not profound. We have already raised questions about the legitimacy of Robinson's use of Bonhoeffer's ideas.[1]

Like Robinson, the radical God-is-dead movement appealed to the "later" Bonhoeffer for the use of some of his terms and operated under the guise of fulfilling Bonhoeffer's proposal for a "religionless Christianity." The attempt to build a theology without the God-hypothesis has not been widely accepted as a positive contribution to theology. Certainly great value has come in asking for the meaning and content of the word "God," and the answers have been various. But for Bonhoeffer, Jesus Christ filled the meaning of the word "God."

Disciples often show ambivalent trends in their interpretations of their master, and this is true of Bonhoeffer's. There is the radical stream seen in various degrees in Robinson, Hamilton, Van Buren, and others, who have appealed predominantly to the themes and suggestions in the popular *Letters and Papers from Prison*, or perhaps the "later Bonhoeffer." The opposite trend appeals to the "whole Bonhoeffer," to his complete works. Falling into this category are Bethge (the close friend of Bonhoeffer and perhaps the man who understands Bonhoeffer best of all), Moltmann, Godsey, Phillips, and others. These interpreters defend Bonhoeffer against being misused for "radical" interpretations. Bethge, because of his influence and importance in this camp, will probably remain the most important interpreter.

Questions might be raised about the restlessness within the church and the self-criticism it has directed against itself in the last decade. The grass roots always furnishes a certain amount of discontent with denominational structures, barren religiosity, and "status-quoism" within the religious culture. Although no sociological gauge to determine cause-effect relations can be established, Bonhoeffer has helped the church's leadership to become critically aware of shortcomings. The popularity of Bonhoeffer in the early sixties among the religiously oriented college student, the reading layman, and the perceptive pastor give some basis for a commentary on the criticism of the church in that decade and which still spills over into this one.

Whatever the ultimate outcome for Bonhoeffer in the history of doctrine and the history of the modern church, his name is certainly one of influence. Because of his ability to say things in a new and pungent way there has been ignited an exciting exchange of ideas in theological literature.

AREAS OF SIGNIFICANCE

In specific areas of theology Bonhoeffer has made several contributions.

1. The church has an important place in Bonhoeffer's thought. If objectivity were a reality in theological circles, Bonhoeffer's view could conceivably serve as a basis for an ecumenical "happening" between the institutional idea found in Roman Catholicism and the "called out" emphasis of Protestantism. Objectivity could perhaps lead Roman Catholic theologians to see that formal institutionalism is alien to the New Testament while voluntaristic Protestants might see that the mystical body of Christ has "space" in the world and is where Jesus Christ is to be found. But since theological wheels move slowly and reevaluation of respective positions seldom occur, the possibilities of Bonhoeffer's position may have to wait for a long time.

Yet the church has possibilities as it contemplates the ecumenical movement. Roman Catholicism is attracted to Bonhoeffer in a way that it is not attracted to the other names of Protestant theology. We have already mentioned that one of the better works on Bonhoeffer comes from a Roman Catholic. William Kuhns remarks that Bonhoeffer's works "speak directly to a Catholic *as* a Catholic, despite their emergence from the most vital sources in Protestant tradition." [2] *The Cost of Discipleship* is akin to works on the spiritual life found in Roman Catholic seminaries and monasteries. *Life Together* "is recognized by many Catholics as the finest available description of living Christian community." [3] *Ethics* has an appeal for it speaks of a "Church which Catholics can recognize and understand. . . ." [4]

Kuhns delineates five areas in Bonhoeffer's thought that hold particular fascination for Roman Catholics: (1) "his idea of community" (the church is the community where Christ is); (2) "his search for the true nature of the Church's authority" (in the concrete situations facing the church who can speak with authority about wrong or right?); (3) "his anthropology" (what is it to be Christian in the modern world? and Bonhoeffer's answer of holy worldliness, or his hope of full manhood); (4) "his effort to forge a dynamic definition of the Church" (the church is defined in relationship to the world); and (5) "his struggle toward a deeply relevant Christology" (the Incarnation becomes the central issue of all facets of theology). [5]

The Protestant likewise shares a deep interest in these five areas. Bonhoeffer attracts Protestants because of his deep respect for the authority of Scripture in determining the idea of the Christian community, the meaning of the Incarnation, the role of the church in the modern world and in the life of modern man come of age.

Bonhoeffer did not forge a union of churches. He criticized the ecumenical movement for its inadequate theology of ecumenicity, and this criticism remains valid today. Certainly

there has been no strong theology of ecumenicity set forth
that refrains from watering down doctrine and swallowing up
weaker denominations. The attitude of the so-called "ecu-
maniac" (somebody else's church is better than mine) was
not the attitude of Bonhoeffer.

Bonhoeffer sought one important thing from the ecumenical movement: a strong denunciation of the apostate church
under Hitler's control. He felt that the church should speak
out on vital issues, even chancing that it may be wrong. This
problem is unsolved in American ecumenicity even when the
National Council of Churches attempts to speak in behalf of
its members. "Who speaks for the churches?" is today an
open question.

2. *Ethics* remains as a powerful work confronting modern
man. We have yet to reckon with many of its features. His
treatment of the role of the Christian in the modern world
will probably be a continuing inspiration for many people if
the prestige of the church continues to diminish.

The new beginning point of ethics is yet to be reckoned with
by philosophical ethics. Nicolas Berdyaev declared that ethics
should teach a man how to die, but philosophical ethics is not
concerned with this. Bonhoeffer answers Berdyaev's question
by declaring ethics' goal for man as being restored to unity
with God. In restoration man becomes real man. Right and
wrong are not products of man's mind but are found only in
the will of God.

Certain emphases in *Ethics* are important because of the
frequent world-denying attitude among Protestants. This is
God's world, created and sustained by him, and man is to
accept it with all its hopes and possibilities as a gift of God.
The narrow view of some Protestants that the world is the
devil's is to insult God's grace and redemptive act. Bonhoeffer
calls us to regain an appreciation for God's world and redemption in it.

The mandates—labor, marriage, government, and the

church—reaffirm the goodness and purpose of life. Could Bonhoeffer be read seriously by some of our deeply discontented students and others, he would no doubt beckon them to a better understanding of themselves in their split world.

3. About the spiritual life, Bonhoeffer has remarkable insights. Those who knew Bonhoeffer found that the development of the spiritual life as he outlined it was not exciting to begin with, but as time passed they reassessed their views and came to regard their six-month stay in the Finkenwalde experiment as a high point of their lives. Bonhoeffer is highly relevant to the needs of modern man in his pursuit of spiritual growth. Here is the source of the church's possibility of being the church in the world, the Christian being the man for other men.

In the context of the Finkenwalde experiment, there may be found some possibilities of rethinking contemporary theological education. The modern seminary *can* be a time-killer in the seminarian's drive for a degree in theology (his union card) without ever helping him to become a theologian or develop a discipline of the spiritual life. The experiment at Finkenwalde produced a host of pastors who stood firm in their purpose to minister in any way possible. The modern seminary turns out men who have not developed a spiritual existence within themselves and are dedicated to serving where the money is the highest. They drift from church to church, lacking vital spirituality, unable to build the churches up because they are empty. The practical and professional emphasis in the seminary has been in the direction of administration, social work, and ecclesiastical machinery rather than the practical discipline of the spiritual life.

4. Christology stands out as the central feature in Bonhoeffer. With one stroke he cut down the controversies centering around the Incarnation. We are concerned with Who, not how in the Incarnation. This is true in the church also. We cannot ask the question "How is Christ in the church?" but "Who

speaks to us in the church?" Doctrine was important for Bonhoeffer. He was not a narrow doctrinaire creature who could
not allow doctrinal differences, but eventually doctrine became
a life and death issue in the Confessing Church's struggle in
Germany. The issue was as important as the survival of the
church. Doctrine is that important. Christology is the center
of doctrine. His controversial utterance, "Whoever knowingly
separates himself from the Confessing Church in Germany
separates himself from salvation," stressed both the importance of doctrine as well as the idea that separation from the
church is equal to cutting oneself off from Christ who exists
in the church.

5. We would like to conclude this work with a word about
Bonhoeffer's face toward the future. Bonhoeffer knew that the
evil of Hitler would one day meet its end and there must be
people who were ready for picking up the pieces. The church
must be ready to minister. In 1942, Bonhoeffer met a few
friends at Werder, and among them was Werner von Haeften,
who was a staff lieutenant of the Army High Command. In
discussing his duties, he asked of Bonhoeffer: "Shall I shoot?
I can get inside the Führer's headquarters with my revolver.
I know where and when the conferences take place. I can get
access." [6]

Bonhoeffer discussed this issue at length. He noted that
ridding the world of Hitler was not everything, for worse
could come by others; but it should accomplish something;
there should be "a change of circumstances, of the government . . . the 'thereafter' had to be so carefully prepared." [7]

In conversations with others, plans were made on various
levels for the possible reconstruction of Germany. Earlier
Bonhoeffer had returned from the safety of New York to give
himself the right to participate in that reconstruction along
with his suffering people. His look toward the future only
expressed his continuing faith in God who was incarnated in
Jesus Christ and the church. In these troubled times plans
need to be made for the future.

Footnotes

CHAPTER I

1. Dietrich Bonhoeffer, *Letters and Papers from Prison*, trans. Reginald Fuller, rev. ed. (New York: The Macmillan Co., 1967), p. 179.

2. Mary Bosanquet, *The Life and Death of Dietrich Bonhoeffer* (London: Hodder and Stoughton, 1968), p. 45.

3. Ibid.

4. Ibid., p. 60.

5. Ibid., p. 89.

6. Ibid., p. 101.

7. Dietrich Bonhoeffer, *No Rusty Swords* (New York: Harper & Row, 1965).

8. Cf. Karl Barth, *Die christliche Dogmatik im Entwurf* (Munich: Chr. Kaiser Verlag, 1927), Vol. IV/1, III/4, III/1, IV/2.

9. *No Rusty Swords*, pp. 237–40.

10. Bosanquet, op. cit., p. 103.

11. *No Rusty Swords*, pp. 182–89.

12. John D. Godsey, *The Theology of Dietrich Bonhoeffer* (Philadelphia: The Westminster Press, 1960), p. 88.

13. Bosanquet, op. cit., p. 174.

14. Maria Von Wedemeyer-Weller in *Bonhoeffer in a World Come of Age*, ed. Peter Vorkink (Philadelphia: Fortress Press, 1968), p. 109.

15. *No Rusty Swords*, pp. 157–73.

16. *Letters and Papers from Prison*, p. xix.

17. Dietrich Bonhoeffer, *The Cost of Discipleship*, trans. R. H. Fuller, rev. ed. (New York: The Macmillan Co., 1960), p. 22.

18. Bosanquet, op. cit., p. 229.

19. Ibid., p. 271.

20. Ibid., p. 272.

21. *I Knew Dietrich Bonhoeffer*, ed. Wolf-Dieter Zimmermann and Ronald Gregor Smith, trans. by Käthe Gregor Smith (New York: Harper & Row, 1966), p. 232.

22. Bosanquet, op. cit., p. 16.

23. Hermeneutics is often defined as the art of interpreting Scripture and therefore deals with principles of interpretation. However, modern usage of the word means the unfolding of the Scripture message in terms of the modern setting.

24. John A. T. Robinson, *Honest to God* (Philadelphia: The Westminster Press, 1963).

25. *Letters and Papers from Prison*, p. 170.

26. Bultmann argues that the world view of the Bible is out of date. It is written in mythical terms, and demythologizing it means that the myth is stripped away to get at the truth embodied in the myth. Cf. Bultmann's essay, "New Testament and Mythology," in *Kerygma and Myth*, ed. Hans Bartsch (New York: Harper & Row, 1961), p. 3.

27. Paul M. Van Buren, *The Secular Meaning of the Gospel* (New York: The Macmillan Co., 1963), p. 133.

28. Thomas J. J. Altizer and William Hamilton, *Radical Theology and the Death of God* (New York: The Bobbs-Merrill Co., 1966), p. 40.

29. Ibid., pp. 116–18.

30. Cf. Alasdair Macintyre, "God and the Theologians," in *The Honest to God Debate*, ed. David L. Edwards (Philadelphia: The Westminster Press, 1963), p. 222.

31. David Jenkins, *Guide to the Debate About God* (Philadelphia: The Westminster Press, 1966), p. 100.

32. Ibid., p. 104.

33. Eberhard Bethge, *Dietrich Bonhoeffer*, trans. Eric Mosbacher, et al. (New York: Harper & Row, 1970). Cf. also E. Bethge, "The Challenge of Dietrich Bonhoeffer's Life and Theology," *World Come of Age*, ed. Ronald Gregor Smith (Philadelphia: Fortress Press, 1967).

34. Jürgen Moltmann and Jürgen Weissbach, *Two Studies in the Theology of Bonhoeffer*, trans. Reginald H. Fuller and Ilse Fuller (New York: Charles Scribner's Sons, 1967).

35. Ibid.

36. See note 12.

37. Ecclesiology, or the doctrine of the church and the nature of its existence as the body of Christ.

38. John A. Phillips, *Christ for Us in the Theology of Dietrich Bonhoeffer* (New York: Harper & Row, 1967).

39. William Kuhns, *In Pursuit of Dietrich Bonhoeffer* (Garden City: Doubleday, Image Books, 1969).

40. Phillips, op. cit., p. 27.

41. William B. Gould, *The Worldly Christian* (Philadelphia: Fortress Press, 1967).

CHAPTER II

1. *The Communion of Saints*, trans. Ronald Gregor Smith, et al. (New York: Harper & Row, 1963).

2. Following the example of Martin E. Marty, ed., in *The Place of Bonhoeffer* (New York: Association Press, 1962).

3. Peter Berger is quick to point out that Bonhoeffer's definition declares itself for an empirical approach, but the argument is carried forth on an abstract, not an empirical approach to sociology. Cf. *The Place of Bonhoeffer*, p. 59.

4. *The Communion of Saints*, p. 23.

5. Ibid., p. 24.

6. Ibid., p. 31.

7. Ibid.

8. Ibid.

9. Ibid., p. 36.

10. Ibid., p. 49.

11. Sociologically, the problem of an empirical collective being is untenable.

12. *Communion of Saints*, p. 59.

13. Ibid., p. 57.

14. Ibid., p. 78.

15. Ibid., p. 79.

16. Ibid., p. 81.

17. Ibid., p. 83.

18. Ibid., p. 85.

19. Ibid., p. 97.

20. The view of Max Scheler in *Wertethik*.

21. *Communion of Saints*, p. 100.

22. Ibid. Bonhoeffer's theory that two different concepts of the church exist in the New Testament, a Jerusalem version which is the basis of Roman Catholicism, and a Gentile, Pauline view serving as foundation for Lutheranism, will undoubtedly disturb those of the free church tradition who would not acknowledge this to be true.

23. *The Communion of Saints*, p. 101.

24. Ibid., p. 103.

25. Ibid., p. 115.

26. Ibid., p. 130.

27. Ibid., p. 137.

28. Ibid., p. 139.

29. Ibid., p. 151.

30. Ibid., p. 154. The "gathered-church" is one stressing voluntary commitment, while the *Volkskirche* is one that involves membership by infant baptism.

31. *The Communion of Saints*, p. 156.
32. Ibid., p. 169.
33. Ibid., p. 173.
34. Ibid., p. 175.
35. Ibid., p. 185.
36. Bonhoeffer says that "pure" doctrine is not a condition for the existence of the congregation of the saints (Isa. 55:11 says nothing of this), p. 187. This verse is often quoted by Bonhoeffer, and it is strange that in this context an Old Testament verse should be used to delineate what the church should or should not be, especially since he emphasizes the kingdom of Christ as opposed to the kingdom of God.
37. *The Communion of Saints*, p. 193.
38. Eschatology is the doctrine of the end of the age, or the consummation of all things. It has a broad meaning describing the beginning of life in Christ *now*, but here it concerns the church's future at Christ's return.
39. *The Communion of Saints*, p. 200.
40. Ibid., p. 204.

CHAPTER III

1. Dietrich Bonhoeffer, *Act and Being*, trans. Bernard Noble (New York: Harper & Row, 1961), p. 30.
2. Ibid., p. 39.
3. Ibid., p. 41.
4. Ibid.
5. Ibid.
6. Ontology is an area of philosophy that examines the nature of being, or reality. What does it mean to be? What is existence?
7. Ibid., p. 51.
8. Ibid., p. 52.
9. Cf. Quentin Lauer, *Phenomenology: Its Genesis and Prospect* (New York: Harper & Row, Torchbook, 1965), pp. 65–81.
10. *Act and Being*, p. 65.
11. Ibid., p. 69.
12. Ibid., p. 72.
13. Ibid., p. 70.
14. Ibid., p. 83.
15. Ibid., p. 105.
16. Ibid., p. 108.
17. Ibid., pp. 111-12.
18. Ibid., p. 115.
19. Ibid., p. 120. Bonhoeffer appeals to Scripture for several statements like this one. See I Cor. 12:12; 6:15; 1:13; Rom. 6:13, 19; Eph. 2:14. "The Church is the body of Christ: I Cor. 12:12ff.; Rom. 12:4ff.; Eph. 1:23; 4:15f.; Col. 1:18. Christ is in the communion as the communion is in Christ: I Cor. 1:30; 3:16; II Cor. 6:16; 13:5; Col. 2:17; 3:11. The communion is a corporate person whose name is also Christ: Gal. 3:28; Col. 3:10f.; cf. Eph. 1:23" (pp. 120–21).

20. Ibid., p. 124. 22. Ibid., p. 128.
21. Ibid., p. 125. 23. Ibid., p. 134.
24. One of the concerns of *Act and Being* is the theology of Barth, which Bonhoeffer regarded as an "act" theology. Barth changed his position considerably, perhaps under the criticism of Bonhoeffer.

25. Ibid., p. 155. 29. Ibid., p. 179.
26. Ibid., p. 163. 30. Ibid., p. 182.
27. Ibid., p. 165. 31. Ibid., p. 111.
28. Ibid., p. 166.

CHAPTER IV

1. Dietrich Bonhoeffer, *Christ, the Center*, trans. John Bowden (New York: Harper & Row, 1966), p. 37.

2. Ibid., p. 40. 8. Ibid., p. 60.
3. Ibid., p. 43. 9. Ibid.
4. Ibid., pp. 49–52. 10. Ibid., p. 64.
5. Ibid., p. 54. 11. Ibid., p. 66.
6. Ibid., p. 55. 12. Ibid., p. 67.
7. Ibid., p. 58. 13. Ibid., pp. 71–72.

14. Martin Kähler, *The So-Called Historical Jesus and the Historic Biblical Christ*, trans. Carl Braaten (Philadelphia: Fortress Press, 1964).

15. Doceticism denied the real manhood of Jesus while the Ebionites denied his divinity. The monophysites regarded the divine and human as merged into a third entity, while the Nestorians hardly admitted a union of the divine and human natures of Jesus Christ.

16. *Christ the Center*, p. 93. Thus one could say that "the man (Jesus) is God and that God is man" (pp. 94–95).

17. Ibid., p. 95.

18. Ibid., p. 109.

19. *Creation and Fall*, trans. John C. Fletcher (New York: The Macmillan Co., 1959). (In same volume with *Temptation*.)

20. Marcion was one of the first to draw up a list of accepted Scriptures of the New Testament. He rejected the Old Testament and regarded the God of the Old Testament as different from the God of the New Testament.

21. *Creation and Fall*, p. 20.

22. Ibid., p. 23. 25. Ibid., p. 17.
23. Ibid., p. 25. 26. Ibid., p. 34.
24. Ibid., p. 29. 27. Ibid., p. 39.

28. Ibid., p. 50.

29. Ibid.

30. Ibid., p. 48.

31. Ibid., p. 52.

32. Ibid., p. 53.

33. Ibid., p. 62.

34. Ibid., p. 65.

35. Ibid., p. 73.

36. Ibid., p. 76.

37. Ibid., p. 77.

38. Ibid., p. 62.

39. Ibid., p. 78.

40. Ibid., pp. 78–79.

41. Ibid., p. 79.

42. Ibid., p. 81.

43. Ibid., pp. 83ff.

44. *Temptation,* trans. Kathleen Downham (New York: The Macmillan Co., 1959). (In same volume with *Creation and Fall.*)

45. Ibid., pp. 101–102.

46. Ibid., p. 102.

47. Ibid., p. 103.

48. Ibid., p. 106.

49. Ibid., p. 107 (italics his).

50. Ibid., p. 109.

51. Ibid., pp. 112–13.

52. Ibid., p. 115.

53. Ibid., pp. 118–19.

CHAPTER V

1. Dietrich Bonhoeffer, *Life Together,* trans. John W. Doberstein (New York: Harper & Bros., 1954).

2. Ibid., p. 21.

3. Ibid., p. 35.

4. Ibid., p. 37.

5. Ibid., p. 39.

6. Ibid., p. 44.

7. The imprecatory psalms are those in which the psalmist prays that God will judge his enemies and in their destruction vindicate the psalmist for his faithfulness.

8. Ibid., p. 46.

9. Ibid., p. 48.

10. Ibid., p. 54.

11. Ibid., p. 54.

12. Ibid., p. 60.

13. Ibid., p. 66.

14. Ibid., p. 77.

15. Ibid., p. 89.

16. Ibid., p. 91.

17. Ibid., p. 94.

18. Ibid., pp. 86–97.

19. Ibid., p. 99.

20. Ibid., p. 100.

21. Ibid., p. 105.

22. Ibid., p. 107.

23. Ibid., p. 110.

24. Ibid., p. 112.

25. Ibid., p. 119.

26. Ibid., p. 120.

27. Ibid., p. 117.

CHAPTER VI

1. Dietrich Bonhoeffer, *The Cost of Discipleship,* trans. R. H. Fuller, rev. ed. (New York: The Macmillan Co., 1960), p. 30.

2. Ibid.
3. Ibid., p. 36.
4. Ibid., p. 50.
5. Ibid., p. 53.
6. Ibid., p. 54.
7. Ibid., p. 56.
8. Ibid., p. 59.
9. Ibid., p. 49.
10. Ibid., p. 69.
11. Ibid., p. 72.
12. Ibid., p. 74.
13. Ibid., pp. 77–78.

14. Ibid., p. 84.
15. Ibid., p. 88.
16. Ibid., p. 89.
17. Ibid., p. 97.
18. Ibid., p. 98.
19. Ibid., p. 102.
20. Ibid., p. 103.
21. Ibid., p. 111.
22. Ibid., p. 110.
23. Ibid., p. 116.
24. Ibid., p. 128.
25. Ibid., p. 129.

26. *Lex talionis* is the law of retaliation or vengeance popularly known as "an eye for an eye, a tooth for a tooth. . . ."
27. *The Cost of Discipleship*, p. 133.
28. Ibid., p. 142.
29. Ibid., p. 146.
30. Ibid., p. 148.
31. Ibid., p. 152.
32. Ibid., p. 153.
33. Ibid., p. 156, footnote.
34. Ibid., p. 163.
35. Ibid., pp. 165–66. "If it [the Gospel] came in power that would mean that the day of judgment had arrived" (p. 166).
36. Ibid., p. 170.

37. Ibid., p. 174.
38. Ibid.
39. Ibid., pp. 179–98.
40. Ibid., p. 191.
41. Ibid., p. 198.
42. Ibid., p. 201.
43. Ibid., p. 203.
44. Ibid., p. 206.
45. Ibid.
46. Ibid., p. 209.

47. Ibid., p. 210.
48. Ibid., p. 214.
49. Ibid.
50. Ibid., p. 215.
51. Ibid., pp. 215–16.
52. Ibid., pp. 221–22.
53. Ibid., p. 227.
54. Ibid., p. 240.
55. Ibid., p. 234.
56. Ibid., p. 247.

57. Ibid., p. 245. It is not fully clear how Bonhoeffer guards himself against universalism, for Christ took the flesh of all mankind. It seems that *apocatastasis*, or universal salvation, is a temptation to him all along.
58. Ibid., p. 252.
59. Ibid., p. 254.
60. Ibid., p. 264, footnote.

61. Ibid., p. 267.
62. Ibid., p. 266.
63. Ibid., p. 206, footnote; *The Communion of Saints*, p. 152.
64. Ibid., p. 235.
65. Ibid., p. 275.

CHAPTER VII

1. William Kuhns, *In Pursuit of Dietrich Bonhoeffer* (Garden City: Doubleday, Image Books, 1969), p. 130.
2. Dietrich Bonhoeffer, *Ethics*, trans. Neville Horton Smith (New York: The Macmillan Co., 1965), p. 19.
3. Ibid., p. 20.
4. Ibid., p. 24.
5. Ibid., p. 33.
6. Epistemology is the area of philosophy dealing with knowledge, how we know, sources of knowledge, and ways of knowing.

7. Ibid., p. 38.
8. Ibid., p. 40.
9. Ibid., p. 52.
10. Ibid., p. 56.
11. Ibid., p. 63, footnote.
12. Ibid., pp. 65–67.
13. Ibid., pp. 76–77.
14. Ibid., p. 77.
15. Ibid., p. 80.
16. Ibid., p. 84.
17. Ibid., p. 85.
18. Ibid., p. 99.
19. Ibid., p. 100.
20. Ibid., p. 108.
21. Ibid., p. 110.
22. Ibid., pp. 112–16.
23. Ibid., p. 133.
24. Ibid., p. 142.
25. Ibid., p. 144.
26. Ibid., p. 151.
27. Ibid., p. 156.
28. Ibid., p. 167.
29. Ibid., p. 176.
30. Ibid., p. 188.
31. Ibid., p. 197.

32. Ibid., p. 204.
33. Ibid., p. 207.
34. Ibid.
35. Ibid., p. 223.
36. Ibid., p. 225.
37. Ibid.
38. Ibid., p. 233.
39. Ibid., p. 229.
40. Ibid., p. 235.
41. Ibid., p. 236.
42. Ibid., p. 244.
43. Ibid., p. 251.
44. Ibid., p. 252.
45. Ibid., pp. 255–56.
46. Ibid., p. 258.
47. Ibid., p. 277.
48. Ibid., p. 278.
49. Ibid., p. 281.
50. Ibid., p. 283.
51. Ibid., p. 287.
52. Ibid., pp. 292–93, 301–2.
53. Ibid., pp. 296–302.
54. Ibid., p. 313.
55. Ibid.
56. Ibid., pp. 330–31.

57. Ibid., pp. 333–39.
58. Ibid., p. 340.
59. Ibid., pp. 342–44.
60. Ibid., pp. 352–53.
61. Ibid., pp. 355–56.

62. Ibid., p. 371.
63. Ibid., p. 372.
64. Ibid., p. 84.
65. Ibid.
66. Ibid., p. 85.

CHAPTER VIII

1. Dietrich Bonhoeffer, *Letters and Papers from Prison*, ed. Eberhard Bethge, trans. Reginald Fuller and others, rev. ed. (New York: The Macmillan Co., 1967).
2. Ibid., pp. 1–4. There is a similar treatment in chapter III of *Ethics*.

3. Ibid., p. 9.
4. Ibid.
5. Ibid., p. 17.
6. Ibid.
7. Ibid., pp. 25–32.
8. Cf. pp. 139, 184.
9. Ibid., p. 139.
10. Ibid., p. 142.
11. Ibid.
12. Ibid., p. 164.
13. Ibid., p. 168.
14. Ibid., p. 169.
15. Ibid., p. 188.

16. Ibid., p. 193.
17. Ibid., p. 193.
18. Ibid., p. 204.
19. Cf. ibid., p. 123.
20. Ibid., pp. 150–51.
21. Ibid., p. 176.
22. Ibid.
23. Ibid., pp. 180–83.
24. Ibid., p. 190.
25. Ibid., pp. 153–62.
26. Ibid., p. 161.
27. Ibid., p. 200.
28. Ibid., p. 225.

CHAPTER IX

1. See chapter I.
2. Kuhns, op. cit., p. 258.
3. Ibid.
4. Ibid.
5. Ibid., pp. 260ff.
6. *I Knew Dietrich Bonhoeffer*, p. 191.
7. Ibid.

Selected Bibliography

I. WORKS BY BONHOEFFER

Act and Being. Translated by Bernard Noble. New York: Harper and Brothers, 1962.

Christ, the Center. Translated by John Bowden. New York: Harper and Row, 1960.

The Communion of Saints. Translated by Ronald Gregor Smith, et al. New York: Harper & Row, 1963.

The Cost of Discipleship. Translated by R. H. Fuller. 2d. ed., rev. New York: The Macmillan Co., 1960. Also available in a Macmillan paperback edition.

Creation and Fall; Temptation. Translated by John C. Fletcher and Kathleen Downham respectively. New York: The Macmillan Co., Macmillan paperback edition, 1959.

Ethics. Translated by Neville Horton Smith. New York: The Macmillan Co., 1955.

I Loved This People. Translated by Keith R. Crim. Richmond, Va.: John Knox Press, 1965.

Letters and Papers from Prison. Edited by Eberhard Bethge. Translated by Reginald Fuller. Rev. ed. New York: The Macmillan Co., 1967.

Life Together. Translated by John W. Doberstein. New York: Harper and Brothers, 1954.

No Rusty Swords. Edited by Edwin Robertson. Translated by John Bowden. New York: Harper and Row, 1965.

The Way to Freedom. Edited by E. H. Robertson. Translated by E. H. Robertson and John Bowden. New York: Harper and Row, 1967.

II. WORKS ABOUT BONHOEFFER

BETHGE, EBERHARD. *Dietrich Bonhoeffer.* Translated by Eric Mosbacher, et al. New York: Harper & Row, 1970.

BOSANQUET, MARY. *The Life and Death of Dietrich Bonhoeffer.* London: Hodder and Stoughton, 1968.

GODSEY, JOHN D. *Preface to Bonhoeffer.* Philadelphia: Fortress Press, 1965.

————. *The Theology of Dietrich Bonhoeffer.* Philadelphia: The Westminster Press, 1960.

GOULD, WILLIAM BLAIR. *The Worldly Christian.* Philadelphia: Fortress Press, 1967.

HAMILTON, KENNETH. *Life in One's Stride.* Grand Rapids: Wm. B. Eerdmans, 1968.

JENKINS, DAVID E. *Guide to the Debate about God.* Philadelphia: The Westminster Press, 1966.

KUHNS, WILLIAM. *In Pursuit of Dietrich Bonhoeffer.* Garden City: Doubleday, Image Books, 1969.

MARLE, RENÉ. *Bonhoeffer.* Translated by Rosemary Sheed. New York: Newman Press, 1968.

MARTY, MARTIN E., ed. *The Place of Bonhoeffer.* New York: Association Press, Seminary Paperbacks, 1962.

MARTY, MARTIN, and PEERMAN, DEAN, eds. *A Handbook of Christian Theologians.* New York: World Publishing Co., 1967.

MOLTMANN, JÜRGEN, and WEISSBACH, JÜRGEN. *Two Studies in the Theology of Bonhoeffer.* Translated by Reginald H. Fuller and Ilse Fuller. New York: Charles Scribner's Sons, 1967.

PHILLIPS, JOHN A. *Christ for Us in the Theology of Dietrich Bonhoeffer.* New York: Harper & Row, 1967.

ROBERTSON, E. H. *Dietrich Bonhoeffer.* Richmond, Va.: John Knox Press, 1966.

SMITH, R. GREGOR, ed. *World Come of Age.* Philadelphia: Fortress Press, 1967.

VORKINK, II, PETER, ed. *Bonhoeffer in a World Came of Age.* Philadelphia: Fortress Press, 1968.

ZIMMERMANN, WOLF-DIETER, and SMITH, RONALD GREGOR, eds. *I Knew Dietrich Bonhoeffer.* Translated by Käthe Gregor Smith. New York: Harper & Row, 1964.